Southern Living. GARDEN GUIDE

Landscaping

Series Editor: Lois Trigg Chaplin

Text by William Slack

Oxmoor House.

Contents

Library of Congress Catalog Number: 96-71089
ISBN: 0-8487-2251-5
Manufactured in the United States of America
Second Printing 1999

We're Here for You!
We at Oxmoor House are dedicated to serving you
with reliable information that expands your imagination and enriches your life. We welcome your
comments and suggestions. Please write us at:

Oxmoor House, Inc.
Editor, LANDSCAPING Garden Guide
2100 Lakeshore Drive
Birmingham, AL 35209

Editor-in-Chief: Nancy Fitzpatrick Wyatt
Editorial Director, Special Interest Publications:
Ann H. Harvey
Senior Editor, Editorial Services: Olivia Kindig Wells
Art Director: James Boone

Southern Living Garden Guide
LANDSCAPING

Series Editor: Lois Trigg Chaplin
Assistant Editor: Kelly Hooper Troiano
Copy Editor: Anne S. Dickson
Editorial Assistant: Allison D. Ingram
Garden Editor, *Southern Living*: Linda C. Askey
Indexer: Katharine R. Wiencke
Concept Designer: Eleanor Cameron
Designer: Carol Loria
Illustrator: Kelly Davis
Senior Photographer, *Southern Living*: Van Chaplin
Production Director: Phillip Lee
Associate Production Manager: Vanessa C. Richardson
Production Assistant: Faye Porter Bonner

Our appreciation to the staff of *Southern Living*
magazine for their contributions to this book.

Cover: *Foxgloves (back) and Pansies (front)*
Frontispiece: *Impatiens, palmetto, and live oaks
(front to back)*

Scilla

Hostas and rhododendron

Landscaping Primer

When it's all done, a well-designed landscape will be one that you can enjoy from indoors, too.

Landscaping. Just the very word brings images of beautiful lawns, artful flowerbeds, and well-placed trees and shrubs.

Designing and landscaping your own property can be exciting, rewarding, and inspiring. But it can also seem overwhelming. Most people ask these questions: Where do I begin? How much know-how do I need? How much will it cost?

This book takes the mystery out of creating a landscape plan. Beautiful gardens are simply the result of a logical process. Each section simplifies the steps of landscape design and provides a how-to road map for garden planning. By blending natural and man-made elements, you can personalize your property and transform a ho-hum yard into the garden spot of the neighborhood. Use this book to create an inviting and useful living environment—an outdoor room, so to speak. Imagine that the tree canopy with its leaves and limbs provides a ceiling. Fences, walls, hedges, or buildings form the walls, and the paving, lawn, or ground cover acts as the flooring and carpeting.

In the following pages, you will discover that landscaping is more than just planting a shrub next to the front door. It is a logical process that evolves easily from one phase to the next. Assess your needs, and then make a wish list of what you want in your landscape. As you analyze your property, look at all the positives and negatives of the existing landscape. Next is the fun part. You put your ideas—what you want to change or create—on paper. Changes might include a new driveway, a better walkway to your front door, an herb garden, and new plantings that make your house and landscape more attractive to passersby.

When choosing new plants and deciding how to arrange them in a planting design, you'll consider their mature size, shape, texture, and cultural requirements, such as their need for water and sun (or shade). For help in selecting plants for your landscape, turn to page 68 for more than 100 plant profiles of flowers, ground covers, shrubs, trees, and vines. These profiles will introduce you to the basic needs and the highlights of each plant. Be sure to think about the plant's practical and functional uses as well as its beauty. Study the photographs carefully, as they show examples of how to use the plants.

Keep in mind as you design your landscape that it will constantly evolve. A landscape changes from year to year, season to season, even day to day. Your landscape will be an ongoing, enjoyable project that provides long-term benefits and lets you express your creativity.

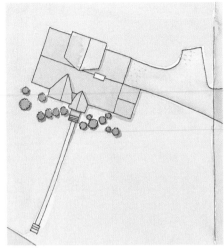

Before any improvements were made on the property at left, a straight walkway and narrow drive to the busy side street made access to the house difficult. Guests had to either park at the front and use the walkway or park in the driveway and step over a retaining wall. Landscaping around the house was scattered.

At first, the job of designing a landscape can seem daunting, but the step-by-step process outlined on the following pages will make the job easier.

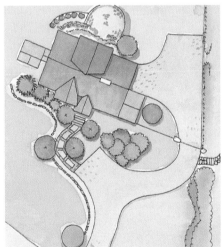

The new plan called for closing off the side entrance, redirecting the driveway to the front street, creating convenient parking for guests, and adding a curved front walkway. The final step was to landscape the property.

5

Your Landscaping Needs

When planning a landscape design, let the architecture of your house influence the style of the garden structures.

As you take a close look at your landscape and consider the kinds of improvements that you want to make, you'll realize that you must first make some general decisions. The landscape style you want and the kind of help you will need to achieve this look are two top priorities in the initial planning.

First, you must decide on a landscape style, be it formal, informal, or exotic. A landscape style affects the feel of a garden, just as a decor determines the atmosphere of a home's interior—in fact, the two should be compatible. And just as you may seek professional advice when redecorating your home, you may want to find the right professional help when planning your new landscape. If you think through these needs at the outset, you will be able to set a realistic budget and a timetable to get things done.

Assessing your landscape needs and finding the people who can advise you, if needed, is essential to the success of your project.

Assessing Your Landscape

There are almost as many ways to landscape a home as there are homeowners. You will want to create a landscape style for your property that reflects your tastes and your home's architecture.

As you continue assessing your landscaping needs, keep in mind how each area is used. It is important to think of your landscape in three categories: public, private, and service. Although this may seem academic, it will help you organize your ideas as you work toward the landscaping style you want to achieve.

Whether determined by yourself or a professional, a good design begins by analyzing your site and your needs.

Landscape Styles

At the beginning of your project, decide what overall style or type of landscape design best suits your tastes and your property. Some factors influencing your decision include the type of neighborhood you live in and the architecture of your home. Do you live in a formal subdivision or a restored neighborhood in a historic district? Or do you live on a dirt road in the country? Your landscape should blend with the personality of its surroundings. The degree of formality of your home will dictate how you landscape, too. You would landscape a rustic log cabin differently than you would a two-story brick mansion or a clapboard Cape Cod cottage.

Also consider your family's lifestyle. If no one in your home enjoys working in the yard, a low-maintenance, easy-care landscape is more practical. A labor-intensive yard, however, with a large lawn, flowerbeds, and herb and vegetable gardens might be tailor-made for a family of gardening enthusiasts.

Here are some popular styles of landscape design.

The Open Lawn. The open lawn is a traditional residential landscape design, popular in cities and in suburbs. It's usually somewhat formal, with emphasis on plantings that simply make the house look good from the street. Trees and shrubs are commonly used to frame the house, and shrub beds often delineate property lines. With this style, the front yard is often a passive area that is used primarily as a pass-through to the front door.

The Courtyard. Private courtyards are a formal landscape style popular for smaller yards, such as those often found in cities. With this style, some or all of the front yard is enclosed for privacy. The courtyard serves as an outdoor room you pass through before entering the house. It is often used as a sitting area or small, private garden. Since courtyards are usually small, with generous areas of paving and limited numbers of plants, maintenance is minimal. Courtyards in the back of the property can be extensions of the house, with large glass doors opening into the walled outdoor room.

A traditional landscape style incorporates an open lawn with a foundation planting of evergreens.

The intimate space of a courtyard creates another room.

7

A meadowlike natural landscape works well on open sites.

The Natural Landscape. Informal landscapes are especially successful on wooded lots, often relying on existing or native plants rather than on new plants. If you have a sunny, open site, this style can be striking.

With this design, very little of the site is disturbed during construction. The natural landscape makes use of existing vegetation and involves little grading, keeping maintenance and costs at a minimum. If lawns are incorporated as part of the design, they are usually limited in size.

The natural landscape is much easier to achieve if you are building a house on an undisturbed lot rather than working around an existing home.

The Combination Garden Landscape. Most people combine different landscape styles. You can create some beautiful landscape effects by combining two or more dissimilar types of design. For example, you may have a formal, open-lawn style in the front of the house, and an informal, natural area along the sides. In the back, you may strive for the more whimsical look of a cottage garden. By combining landscape styles, you can adapt designs to almost any type of architecture.

Combining different landscape styles can create exciting results as you pass from a natural area to a formal one.

The Three Areas of the Landscape

As you begin the design process, remember that most home landscapes can be divided into three basic areas—public, private, and service—each with a specific purpose and function. Although these areas are not always clearly defined, visualizing your yard in this way will help you organize ideas.

Public Area. The part of the property in full view of passersby is called the public area. This is usually the front yard, but on corner lots, it may also include parts of the side yard and even the backyard. Many people give the greatest attention to the public area because it is highly visible.

When designing a landscape plan and deciding what to plant where, take the time to stand back and analyze the front yard from a distance. View it from the street, as most people do. From that distance, think of how you can best show off and complement the house. Remember that simple designs are usually the best, as they enhance rather than compete for attention with the residence.

Also consider how the entire landscape will be seen. Family members will view it from inside, while neighbors will see it from the sidewalk or from a moving car. Avoid concentrating on only one spot at a time, moving from one location to another around the house. Instead, look at the big picture in order to visualize how the different parts will come together. Looking at the property as a whole will give you a sense of continuity and will help you avoid creating a segmented landscape with individual "pockets" of plants.

Private Area. The private area is the part of your lot that is out of public view. Often, it is the backyard—the place where you do most of your outdoor living. How you use it depends on your family's lifestyle and the limitations of the site. The private area includes items of play or relaxation, such as a deck, a patio, a swimming pool, a children's swing set, a vegetable garden, a barbecue grill, or even a hammock. You entertain, play, and relax here.

Even a small backyard can serve as an intimate sanctuary. Its use, however, may change over time, reflecting your family's current needs. For example, a play area once used by small children can later be converted to a flower garden. The backyard may also be redesigned to reduce maintenance.

If you live on a corner lot, you can create your own private area by planting an evergreen screen.

The walled entry gives a feeling of enclosure to this front yard or "public" area.

The private area is a place to congregate, play, work, and relax.

The service area can be functional as well as attractive.

Here, an old garage is transformed into a workable but handsome structure that is now more useful.

Service Area. The service area is the working, or utility, area of your property. Items in a service area include garbage cans, outdoor air-conditioning units, tool storage buildings, utility meters, or even a trailer. You might include a vegetable garden or cut flower garden that you know you won't maintain as a showcase year-round. Most homes have at least a small service area next to the garage or the carport or near the side entrance. If this area is in the open, you'll want to screen it from view.

If you have more than one unsightly view, such as an area where you keep a potting bench or a compost pile, try to consolidate it with other service areas. A single screening is easier, less expensive, and more effective than having several small screened areas.

The type of screen you use depends on such factors as available space, architectural style, and your budget. It can be as simple as a fence, a hedge, or a combination of the two, or it can be as elaborate as a serpentine brick wall.

A Word of Caution. As you begin to plan your next step, remember to keep your design simple. What looks good on paper may in reality result in a crowded landscape. Of the three landscape areas, the front yard is the one people tend to overdo. In

their quest for a beautiful front lawn, some people use too many plants around the house and litter the yard with lawn ornaments.

Before making any changes, consider at least brainstorming your ideas with a professional. The following section discusses the kinds of help available.

Hiring a Professional

One of the first questions to ask yourself when taking on a landscaping project is "Should I do it myself or hire someone to do it for me?" Several factors affect your decision.

One of the most important steps in any good design is a workable drawing. Often this is where you may need to seek advice. A professional designer may help you avoid costly mistakes and come up with fresh ideas. With a planting plan in hand, you can implement the project in stages as money and time are available.

Here are the three basic questions you will first want to ask yourself.

1. How large is the project? If you have an extra-large yard or if you want to landscape the entire lot, the project may seem overwhelming and more than you can handle. Or the property may have special challenges, such as drainage problems, unwanted structures, trees or shrubs that must be removed, or a concrete parking area or wall that must be constructed. In any of these situations, professional assistance is usually worthwhile.

2. What is the budget? The cost of your landscaping project may prove to be very expensive. By doing all or some of the job yourself, you can save a lot of money in labor. Keep in mind, however, that if you need special equipment, hiring a professional (who has the machinery and the operators) may be cheaper and more efficient in the long run than renting the machinery yourself. On a new landscape, a suggested estimate for the cost of the installed project is 10 to 15 percent of the house cost. Structures and paving may increase this percentage.

3. Can professionals do a portion of the work? You may find that you can do some of the work yourself. Landscaping can be completed in phases; it is rarely a problem to divide it into smaller, separate jobs. Working from a master plan, hire professionals to complete the parts of the project that are beyond your ability.

To make a landscape project more affordable, you may enjoy implementing some or all of the plan yourself.

Choosing the right landscape professional can make the difference between a pleasant experience and an unpleasant one.

Who Are the Landscape Professionals?

If you are thinking about hiring a landscape professional for all or part of the project, you will need to know who's who in the business. The three types of landscape professionals are landscape architects, landscape designers, and landscape contractors.

Landscape architects usually have extensive formal training. They are licensed in most states and hold one or more degrees in their field. They design both large commercial projects and residential landscapes. Because of their background and training, landscape architects are probably the most helpful in developing a master plan for your property. They may charge an hourly fee, a lump sum, or a percentage of the construction cost.

Landscape designers generally work on residential landscape projects. They may or may not have the extensive training that landscape architects have. Many are talented garden designers but are prohibited in some states from designing certain structural projects.

Landscape contractors implement the plan. The scope of their work includes grading, paving, planting, installing irrigation systems, and constructing certain structures. Occasionally, landscape architects and landscape designers function as landscape contractors, providing both design and installation services. If you have a completed landscape plan, consider hiring a landscape contractor. Most of them are trained to interpret and implement professionally prepared plans.

Finding the Right Landscape Professional

When looking for a professional landscaper, it helps to be an informed client. Here are some suggestions for proceeding.

• Check the phone book. Call a minimum of three businesses and visit sites to see their work. Talk to their customers.

• Ask around. Most people are willing to share both their positive and negative landscaping experiences.

• Be on the lookout for attractive landscapes. When you see one you admire, ask the homeowners with whom they worked. Most people feel flattered and will happily share their professional's name.

• When interviewing a professional, ask to see samples of his work. Does it suit your style? If not, keep looking.

• When hiring a landscape contractor, always ask if he is certified. Are plants and work guaranteed? Does the total price include soil preparation?

No matter which type of landscape professional you choose, a clear understanding of the scope of the work is important. Each of you must know what is expected of the other. Spell everything out in the agreement. You will probably have to pay a deposit, but don't make the final payment until the project is completed.

The better you communicate your landscaping needs to a professional, the happier you will be with the finished job. To paraphrase a real estate maxim, the three basic principles underlying a satisfactory landscape design are "plan, plan, plan." The following chapters will help you execute your plan in a logical sequence.

When taking on a landscaping project such as this front yard, look at the area as a whole, not in bits and pieces. A good designer will help you think through potential ideas for the property and come up with a workable plan.

This landscape now has a feeling of unity, thanks to a well-designed front yard. A good plan has added to the value and appearance of both the house and the property.

13

Planning Your Landscape Design

Of all the necessary steps in landscape design, planning on paper tops the list.

When you begin work on a landscape design, step back and look at your property through new eyes. (See page 50 for the striking changes made to this landscape.)

When you first begin to think about redesigning your landscape, avoid the temptation of instant design. Don't buy plants on impulse at the garden center just because they are on sale. You first need a well-thought-out landscape plan, or basic blueprint.

Begin by looking at your property through new eyes. If you were seeing it for the first time, what would you like and dislike about the yard? Input from friends, family, or a hired professional, combined with your own ideas, will give you a starting point. See the box on page 21 for a guide to some of the things you'll need to consider. Eventually, all of the items you decide upon will assume final form as the landscape plan.

Preparing a landscape design doesn't have to be complicated if you complete it in these four stages.

- Get accurate measurements to draw a base map (page 15).
- Draw a site analysis (page 17).
- Draw a bubble diagram (page 20).
- Draw the final master plan (page 23).

Begin with a Base Map

Putting your ideas on paper, or "planning with a pencil," is essential to creating a design that you can carry out. To do this, you will need a base map of your existing property that includes accurate measurements. The base map is a scale drawing showing property lines and the placement of the house, garage, sidewalk, and other permanent features on the property. This scale drawing is important because it serves as the foundation for preparing later drawings that will include details of your plan.

When most people are faced with having to prepare an accurate base map with all features drawn to scale, they get concerned about their ability to do this and may even abandon the project. At first glance, the task seems technical and complicated, but it really isn't. If you follow these guidelines, you will see how simple making a base map can be.

Get Accurate Measurements of the Property

To draw your plan to scale, you will need a sketch that shows measurements of the property. You can create your own base map from measurements you take yourself, or you can use the measurements from an existing surveyor's plat.

Using a surveyor's plat. A surveyor's plat shows all your property dimensions and structures (see **Diagram 1**). It usually accompanies your mortgage papers or deed and should be accurate, because it was measured by professional surveyors. If you can't find the surveyor's plat, ask your mortgage company, builder, or city building office for a copy. Review the plat carefully, especially if it's old; you will need to modify it to show items added to or removed from the yard since the plan was drawn. To add items to your surveyor's plat, follow the instructions on measuring your property.

Measuring your property. If you don't have a surveyor's plat, you can measure your property yourself in a couple of hours. (If your lot is extremely large, or if you're not certain where your property lines are, hire a surveyor.) To measure, you will need a 50- or 100-foot tape measure, a sketch pad, a pencil, and a helper. First, use the tape to measure the boundary lines of the property and then record these dimensions. Next, measure the distance from the boundary line to the house. Do this at three or more different points to ensure accuracy. Make a rough sketch of the property and the house on paper and indicate the dimensions. Then, carefully measure and record all

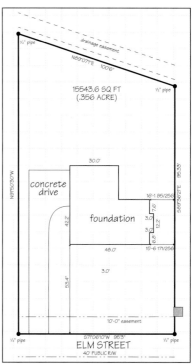

Diagram 1. *A surveyor's plat is the best source for accurate dimensions of your property.*

15

DRAFTING SUPPLIES FOR A BASE MAP

If you plan to draw the base map yourself, the drafting supplies on this list will make the job easier. You can find them at most drafting or art supply stores.

• Four 18- x 24-inch sheets of graph paper. Use paper that is lined to the scale to which you will draw. For example, if you plan to use a scale of 1 inch equals 10 feet, select graph paper with 10 grid squares to the inch. If your base map won't fit on one sheet, tape two or more together. You can also use a smaller scale, such as 1 inch equals 20 feet.
• One roll or 10 sheets of inexpensive tracing paper
• Pencil and eraser
• Engineer's scale*
• 6-inch transparent 45-degree triangle
• Circle template (for trees and shrubs)
• One roll of masking tape or drafting tape
• 2- x 3-foot drafting board*
• 3-foot T square*

*These items are optional, but they make drafting much easier and more efficient.

existing and permanent features (patio, driveway, garage, or other outbuildings) in the yard.

Before completing your sketch, locate all first-floor doors and windows plus any aboveground or belowground utilities. When you are finished, your freehand sketch will include all of the landscape elements, along with accurate dimensions.

Prepare Your Base Map

Now that you have an accurate sketch of your property, you're ready to prepare another drawing—the actual *base map*. You will use the sketch to create a scale drawing of your yard on graph paper. To draw a base map to scale, let 1 inch represent a specific distance. The scale you choose depends on your lot size. A common scale is 1 inch equals 10 feet; for larger lots, allow 1 inch for 20 feet.

Now you're ready to redraw your first working sketch to scale on graph paper, using the recorded measurements. Graph paper is available in 4-, 8- or 10-grid squares per inch. You may need to tape several sheets of graph paper together to have a large enough area to work on. Then tape the sheets to a tabletop. Measure and lightly draw (with a pencil) the lines taken from your base map. (You will darken the lines after everything has been drawn.) Start with the property lines, making sure your entire lot fits on the paper. To make it easier, try using an engineer's scale. This inexpensive drafting tool has different calibrations along each edge. Other helpful items are listed in the adjacent box.

When you complete your base map, you will have an accurate drawing indicating the permanent elements in your yard. These include both man-made items, such as patios and driveways, and natural items, such as trees (see **Diagram 2**). Don't include temporary features, such as a swing set.

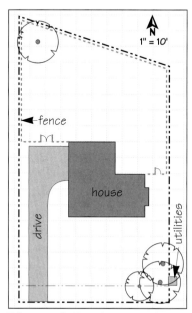

Diagram 2. *Your base map has the dimensions of your lot and shows its physical features.*

Now add two final points of information to your map: Draw and label a north-pointing arrow. (If you aren't sure of the accurate direction, use a compass.) Then, indicate the scale used for your map (for example, 1 inch equals 10 feet). Be sure to put this information at the bottom, top, or sides of the sheet, where it will not interfere with the drawing.

Your base map is now complete. This map will not change. It will serve as a foundation for your site analysis and all future planning. In fact, your base map is such a critical planning tool that you may want to have several copies made before proceeding with your site analysis.

Create a Site Analysis

The next step is to identify the existing conditions in your yard. Designers call this a *site analysis,* which is nothing more than a drawing that marks the existing conditions (see **Diagram 3**). Stand back and analyze your property. No two lots are the same. Your yard is unique; it has its own beauty and its own problems. A careful look will yield several important factors that will influence your design. A site analysis should include anything that affects the experience of being in the garden.

You will need your base map and several sheets of tracing paper to use as overlays with your base map. Using the symbols listed in the adjacent box, make notes directly on the tracing paper about the conditions in your yard. Feel free to add other notes as needed.

Drainage conditions. Is your lot lower than, higher than, or about the same level as the surrounding area? Identify areas in your yard affected by drainage problems. Standing water or erosion are the two most common problems. (See pages 26-28 for information on how to correct drainage problems.)

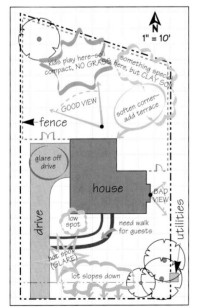

Diagram 3. *A site analysis lists the conditions affecting your property.*

WHAT TO INCLUDE ON A SITE ANALYSIS

Erosion. Label eroded areas with an *E.*

Hot spots or glare. Label extremely hot spots or areas with bad glare *HS.*

Low spots. Label low spots where water tends to gather *LS.*

Noise. If there are any noises that are a problem, such as traffic, write *N* in the area of the source (or spell it out).

Rocks. If you have any rock outcroppings on your property, label them *R.*

Septic tank. If you have a septic tank, label it *ST,* and put a square around it. If possible, indicate where the septic field lines are located.

Shady. Label shady areas *S.*

Steep slopes. Label any steep slopes *SS* at the highest point, with arrows pointing down to the lowest point.

Utilities. Locate any utilities, such as power, telephone, cable, and water, and label them with a *U.* If you don't know the location of any underground utilities, you can call the One Call System service for your state, which will locate them at no cost.

Views. Indicate good views with *GV* and bad views with *BV.*

Winds. Draw directional arrows to indicate the direction of any prevailing winds.

You should also note any wet spots that may need special treatment.

Wind direction. Cooling summer breezes are desirable. However, prevailing winds that bring a chill in the winter or hot, dry air in the summer can be hard on some landscape plants and may increase your utility bills. If you live in an area where there are strong, unwelcomed seasonal winds, place arrows on your site analysis to indicate the direction of the prevailing wind.

Views. Does your next-door neighbor have a beautiful yard and a lovely flower garden? Is there an unsightly view across the street? When designing a landscape plan, remember that there may be some things you want to see and others that you don't want to see. Draw arrows on the map to identify desirable and undesirable views.

Sun and shade. Indicate areas in your yard that receive full sun or heavy shade. This information will help you select plants suitable for sunny and shady conditions.

Existing Plants

Before you begin your landscaping project, you have some decisions to make if you already have plants on your property. You will need to consider four factors when making your decisions about whether to keep existing plants or get rid of them. Once you have made this determination, you should mark on your base map plants that you decide to keep in their original location. (See page 24 for plant symbols.)

You must determine which plants to keep and which ones to remove. In this case, only a large shade tree was kept.

Aesthetics. Plants that look good and are healthy may be worth incorporating into the new design. Is the plant attractive and does it look good in its current location? If the plant is old and thin, with a poor shape because it is diseased or has a lot of dead wood, the decision is easy—it goes. However, if it looks good and is healthy but seems out of place, you have some choices. You can leave the plant alone and incorporate it into a new design; or, if it isn't too big, you can transplant it. Generally, the older the plant, the more difficult it is to relocate. Older plants have more extensive root systems, much of which can be lost in transplanting. If that is the case, make the prized specimen, such as a gnarly old live oak, the focal point of a new landscape design.

Function. In addition to looking pretty, plants also have practical uses. For example, they can provide shade or block wind. Some trees and shrubs are used as privacy screens or as visual buffers. Others frame a view. Plants are also used to control where people walk. Always consider the function plants perform before you remove them.

Sentiment. Certain plants can have sentimental value. A shrub started from cuttings by a loved one or a tree that is so large that it seems almost criminal to remove it, may not be in the ideal spot. However, it's not always easy to say, "Cut down that tree" or "Remove that shrub," because of the special meaning the plant may hold.

Economy. Consider the value of the plant and whether it's worth the trouble to transplant. For example, you may not want to dig up a Heller holly when you can buy a new one for 20 dollars.

Analyze the Circulation

Before designing a planting plan and concentrating on trees, shrubs, grass, and flowers for your yard, take a look at the circulation, or how people (and cars) move around the yard. Is there enough room for cars to operate? Do drivers have to squeeze their car into a parking space and back over the flowerbed to turn the car around? Do visitors have to park on the lawn and then search for the sidewalk that will take them to the front door? You should address these concerns before choosing any plants. The existing driveway, walkways, and other permanent structures should already be marked on your surveyor's plat. If they are not, be sure to add them to your base map. (See pages 29-33 for more information on driveways, parking, and walkways.)

Utilities and Easements

An often-forgotten factor that can affect how you landscape is the utilities. Underground utilities, such as telephone, gas, electric, water, TV cable, septic tank, and sewer lines, can restrict what you plant or construct on top of them. Overhead lines prohibit planting tall-growing trees underneath them.

If you plan on digging but aren't sure where the lines are buried, call One Call System. This multistate network collaborates

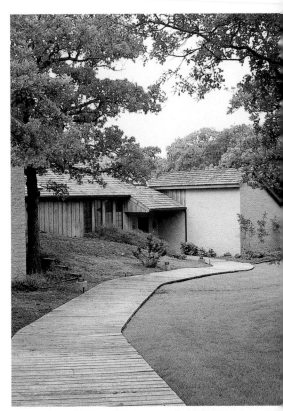

Before you do any planting, analyze the circulation pattern—or means to guide people through your landscape—to see that it's adequate.

Mark the location of underground utility lines before you dig.

When properly planned, a sitting area can be a quiet retreat.

with participating utility companies to check records and to locate and stake out underground lines that might be damaged by digging. You should be aware that in some new subdivisions, the final grading may not be done until after the utilities have been laid underground. This means that the lines may not be as deep as the line locators indicate.

You should also know about any easements that exist on your property. If they are present, they may limit what you do there. Check your deed or property plat for their location. If you're not sure where they are or if you have questions, contact your courthouse or city hall.

You can note utilities on your base map by drawing lines marked with the letters that signify each utility.

The Bubble Diagram

Now that you have a base map and a site analysis, it's time to explore the new landscaping possibilities for your yard. The *bubble diagram* is essentially a sketch that locates places for specific activities.

Make a Wish List

The next step is to determine what you want to include in your landscape. Gather the family and ask what they'd like to add—whether it's a swimming pool, a flower garden, or a play area. Write down everything that comes to mind, letting your imaginations run wild. Some things will be specific, such as a toolshed, while other needs will be general, such as privacy. Cost must be considered at some point, but don't concern yourself with it now. You can make choices later. The box on page 21 lists some of the most common items; you may want to add others.

As you make your wish list, prioritize the items, because your wants and needs may conflict. You should plan to make structural changes, such as walls or walkways, first before installing plants. Think about how you use your house and garden. Which entryways do you use most often? Do you cook out a lot? Where do the children play? How many cars do you need to accommodate? Try to answer any questions you can think of that relate to how you use your outdoor property.

This is also the time to decide how much time or money you are willing to put into maintenance. You don't want to design and build a high-maintenance garden if you are not able to devote the time it takes to maintain it.

After discussing everything with your family, make a final, clean version of your wish list.

Place Function Bubbles

Now the real fun begins. You have a site analysis that includes all of the opportunities and limitations your site presents, and you have a wish list of what you want your new landscape to include. The next step is to put the two together.

While you may be tempted to skip this step—don't! Think of this exercise as creating your outdoor living areas. And just as you wouldn't dare buy expensive appliances for a kitchen you had not yet designed, you don't want to purchase any items for your outdoor rooms without having carefully created a plan. This is your opportunity to make your landscaping dreams come true on paper and to plan exactly what you want in your landscape without actually spending any money on construction.

To start your bubble diagram, tape a fresh piece of tracing paper over your base map. Look at the high-priority items on your wish list, and then look at the base map to see where they might fit in best.

Drawing bubbles helps you to place and size areas for specific activities. Draw bubbles and label them accordingly on the drawing. Continue this all over the map—front yard, side yard, and backyard.

You will likely change and rearrange some of the bubbles several times as you work; if things get messy, simply replace the sheet of tracing paper (see **Diagram 4**).

At this point, concentrate on the big picture and on solving problems. As you decide where to locate areas for activities, remember circulation. People will be moving around the yard, walking from one area to

Diagram 4. *A bubble diagram helps you decide which locations are best for the items on your wish list.*

Sunlight and level ground may influence where you locate a garden.

another. For example, the best route to the children's play area will not be through the vegetable garden and around the dog pen. Be aware of how people will move through the yard as you locate areas for activities.

When you are drawing bubbles and deciding where to locate certain activities, ask yourself some questions. Is that area of your yard level? Is it a sunny or shady location? Can it be seen from the house if it is important to view the area from inside? Are there any utilities that restrict uses in that area? A dog pen, a clothesline, and storage for garbage cans and firewood should be placed in accessible but inconspicuous locations. They are part of the service area discussed on page 10.

Decide on the most convenient and logical area for storage.

Visualize Your Final Look

By better defining the bubbles, you give each area a specific shape. (You may need to go through several sheets of tracing paper before you arrive at what you want.) Think of your yard as a group of outdoor rooms, each one having its own use. As you develop your plan, you will probably experiment with different ways to define the rooms with features such as plants, walkways, fences, patios, and decks.

When deciding on the size and shape of a specific area, consider how much space each activity requires. Whether it's a location for eating, gardening, working, or playing, be careful not to make the area too large or too small. If the space is too large, much of it will be wasted. If it is too small, it may be unusable.

At this stage, you are still developing the general, overall layout of the property. Avoid getting into details. For example, label an area as a shrub bed rather than naming individual plants.

The overall look of your landscape will start to take shape as you work your way around the plan, designing the different areas. And remember, it's much easier to make changes on paper than after the fact. Don't rush this step. You'll be better off extending this process over a few days or weeks because it's such a critical step.

Start Your Master Plan

After refining your bubble diagram, you can begin to firm up your ideas. This step will determine how all the pieces of this landscape puzzle fit together. Before you begin this final stage, be sure to read the chapters that follow for specific information on structures, planting designs, plants, and lawns. Once you have reviewed these basic ideas, you are ready to complete your *master plan* on paper. See the adjoining box for suggestions on consolidating your plans.

Design Permanent Structures

Once you have consolidated your planning sheets to form your working drawing, you are ready to begin drafting your final master plan. You will begin by drawing in the permanent structures, including those already existing on your property and those your new plan calls for. Once these are in place, you're ready to sketch your plantings.

Structural features (see **Diagram 5**). Many professional designers feel that all structural features in the landscape should be located and designed first. Because cars have such a big impact on the landscape, you should design the driveway and parking areas first. Walkways, terraces, decks, and patios should also be designed now.

Diagram 5. *Locate structural items, such as new parking, walkways, fences, and pools.*

Work areas are often made as inconspicuous as possible, but you can turn one into a feature of your design.

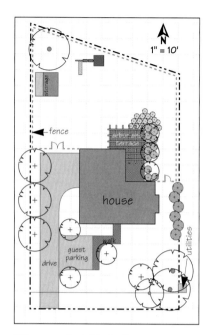

Diagram 6. *Add shade trees and understory trees as well as plants for screening.*

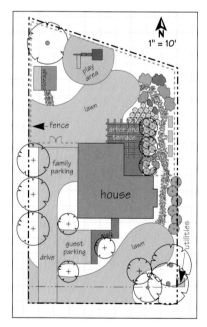

Diagram 7. *Designate specialty areas, such as flower and vegetable gardens.*

Trees and screening (see **Diagram 6**). Trees should be accounted for early in the design process. Be sure to include new as well as existing trees. (See page 57 for more information about trees.)

Specialty areas (see **Diagram 7**). Refer once again to your wish list and add specialty areas, such as vegetable gardens, water features, cold frames and greenhouses, or rose gardens. When you have drawn these in to scale, you should see a free-flowing lawn begin to take shape.

Lawn area. Loosely draw smooth, flowing lines around your house and other permanent features using a pencil. Once you are satisfied with the basic shapes, draw the permanent bed lines. What is left will most likely become lawn. (See page 64 for more information on lawn design.)

Prepare the Planting Areas

Up to now, you have not dealt with any specific plants other than trees and existing plants you intend to keep. However, you are now ready to place the foundation plantings and borders into your evolving master plan.

Foundation planting. Plantings used next to the house should do two things. They should complement the architecture and help direct you to the front door. To learn about designing an effective foundation planting, turn to "Planting Design" beginning on page 48. Then look at the lawn border that you have just drawn on your plan. The areas between your house and the lawn border are where your foundation planting will go.

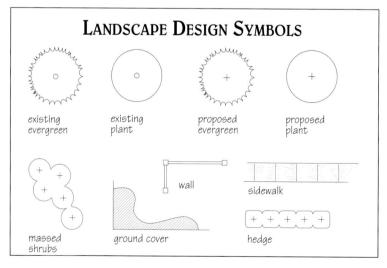

LANDSCAPE DESIGN SYMBOLS

existing evergreen

existing plant

proposed evergreen

proposed plant

massed shrubs

ground cover

wall

sidewalk

hedge

Your next step is to draw symbols representing where plants should be located on your plan. (See the Landscape Design Symbols on page 24.) Don't worry about picking out specific plants now, but do keep in mind how tall and wide each plant should be.

Plant list. Finish up your plan by adding ground covers, border plants, and annual and perennial color. You may want to take another look at your wish list to be sure your master plan has encompassed all the items that you set out to include.

At this point, you should also make a list of all the new plants you want to add to your property, categorized by groups: trees, shrubs, ground covers and vines, and annuals and perennials. This makes shopping a snap. Your plant list should include the common name, botanical name, total quantity, and size of plant to buy. (For more on specific plants and before you make any purchases, refer to "Choosing Trees and Shrubs for Design" beginning on page 56.)

Implement Your Plan

You may be satisfied with the plan as it is on the tracing paper, or you may decide to redraw everything onto a new sheet (see **Diagram 8).** Either way, you will want to make several photocopies of your plan to keep on file.

Before going any further, check the information in the sections on "Planning the Structural Elements" (page 26) and "Planting Design" (page 48). Once you have reviewed these, you can make educated decisions about the time frame, the type of assistance you need, and the actual plants in which you want to invest. Just remember that you've put a lot of work into your master plan, and you will refer to it often during the design stage.

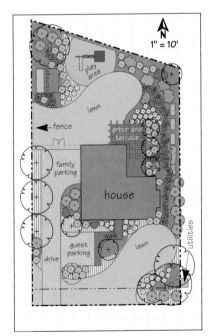

Diagram 8. *Complete your plan by adding foundation plantings, ground covers, and flowers.*

LANDSCAPE DESIGN SCHEDULE

To implement your plan, follow these steps:

- Clean the site by removing unwanted plants and structures.
- Complete any necessary rough grading and leveling.
- Install any large undertakings, such as a swimming pool, or underground projects, such as drainage or irrigation systems or utilities.
- Prepare the soil by tilling and adding amendments.
- Build landscape features and garden amenities. If any items such as walls, play structures, garden ponds, or patios are on a waiting list, keep them in mind as you are planting.
- Complete final grading, making sure your yard drains properly.
- Implement the planting plan. Plant trees first, especially if there is no existing shade, and establish a lawn. These will often help to prevent soil erosion and reduce mud and dust.
- Perform final cleanup and prepare a maintenance schedule.

Planning Structural Elements

Permanent structural elements affect how you move around your property.

You probably give much time and thought to the design and floor plan of your house but seldom think of your yard as having a "floor plan." To many, landscaping is synonymous with planting shrubs around the lawn. But there is more to the landscape than just plants. The structural elements of a landscape, such as driveways, walkways, walls, and fences, determine how a landscape actually functions. However, before you build a driveway or site any landscape structure, you must take into consideration how the property drains. Proper drainage is essential to having an attractive landscape.

Explore Drainage Options

It is crucial to move rainwater away from the house and out of the yard so that water doesn't accumulate in large, standing puddles on the property. However, you don't want to move water so fast that it causes erosion. Before you think about structures and plantings, you must decide how you will move rainwater away from the house and off the property. You then need to incorporate any resulting landscape changes into your overall design. Moving rainwater can be accomplished in several ways.

Grading

Moving soil to produce the correct slope is called grading. It can be as simple as using a shovel or as complicated as bringing in a bulldozer. Unless your yard has major problems, you should be able to do the grading yourself. Sometimes grading is done to accommodate a new landscape feature, such as a driveway or a patio. In this case, the grading will change the way water moves off the property. Always take cases like these into consideration and hire a professional to help with the big jobs.

Grading will affect how water moves across a property. For example, a new driveway will create rainwater runoff that must have a place to go.

Diverting Water

You can often improve the drainage in one area of the yard by channeling standing water in another direction. It's easy to tell if you have a drainage problem—just go into your yard after a heavy rain. If standing water remains for more than 24 hours, you may have a problem. The simplest remedy for moving the water is to create trenches. But before digging, check with your utility companies for the location of any underground pipes, lines, or cables.

On a flat lot, you can change how rainwater drains away by sculpting the terrain. By using mounds of earth called *berms*, you can guide water in a certain direction. In addition to controlling water runoff, berms help provide privacy and add interest and beauty to a flat yard.

Gutter downspouts are the cause of another common drainage problem. Rainwater from the roof pours from the downspout into a plant bed that is usually next to the house. This glut of water can lead to all sorts of plant problems. In a sense, the plants drown.

An inexpensive and easy way to correct this problem is to use plastic pipe. This will take the rainwater and direct it downhill, away from the house. Just slide a PVC pipe over the end of the downspout and bury the remainder of the pipe underground, leaving only the open end exposed.

Make sure downspouts aren't drowning your plants with rainwater.

Preventing Erosion

On steep slopes, water leaving the site too fast may be the problem. Hillside erosion can be exasperating. By slowing the speed of the water runoff, you can usually slow the rate of erosion. You can control erosion on a slope by terracing and grading the landscape or using soil-stabilizing plants, riprap, or retaining walls.

Terracing involves placing what look like large stairsteps down a hill. Terraces are made from stones, railroad ties, concrete, bricks, or treated timbers. They slow the speed of the water and reduce erosion. (See page 37 for more about terracing.)

Grading can be successful when water is redirected elsewhere, perhaps down a more gentle slope. This decreases the amount of runoff and reduces the rate of erosion. An effective method of diverting water is to dig a shallow trench at the top of the hill. Mound earth on the downhill side of the trench, directing the water in the desired direction.

A terraced front yard can have dramatic results and prevent erosion at the same time.

Masses of pachysandra (front) and gumpo azaleas (back) turn a potentially trouble-some slope into an attractive site.

Retaining walls act as dams to hold back soil and can effectively reduce erosion. On steep hillsides, they may be your best choice, despite the expense and engineering challenges involved. They may vary from a simple-to-build, 2-foot-high wall to an 8-foot-high wall that requires heavy construction equipment and professional design expertise. In either case, the level area created by the retaining wall redirects runoff or reduces water speed. The flat area is easier to maintain and provides a level, more usable space.

You can construct walls from a variety of materials, including preformed and poured concrete, rock, railroad ties, treated lumber, brick, and block. Because low retaining walls are cheaper and easier to construct than high ones, some people install a series of low walls down the hill instead of a single high one.

Riprap, a collection of chunks of stones, rocks, or concrete rubble, is sometimes used on hillsides to reduce erosion. When placed on a slope, it slows water flow and encourages soil buildup. The stones and rocks should be at least 6 inches in diameter. Half-bury them in the ground, and, if desired, plant your favorite ground cover among the stones.

Plants can be the easiest and sometimes least expensive method of erosion control. Roots hold and bind the soil, while leaves cushion the force of falling raindrops, reducing "splash erosion." Sometimes lawns are used to stabilize hillsides. However, if the slope is too steep to mow, ground covers, shrubs, and trees are better choices.

Retaining walls can be functional, as well as dramatic, design elements in the landscape.

People and Cars in the Landscape

Always plan for the circulation on your property before doing any planting design and plant selection. If your sidewalks are wide enough, if you have adequate parking space, and if your patio is where you want it, you can start choosing plants. However, if your driveway leads guests straight to the garage instead of the front door, if your walkways are uncomfortably narrow, or if your deck is cramped, you should consider making some changes. Inadequate and poorly designed driveways, parking areas, and walkways are common landscape problems. Unless you are building a new home, the sidewalk and the driveway probably already exist; but you can change their size, if necessary, or move them to better locations.

Driveways

Inadequate parking is especially common in older homes built when most families owned only one car. Even in new homes, cars often end up maneuvering in quarters that are too tight. Regardless of whether you are planning a new driveway or renovating an existing one, here are some minimum space requirements to keep in mind.

The minimum width for a straight, single-car driveway is 10 feet, although 12 feet is better. This gives you ample room to open car doors without bumping anything. A double-car driveway should provide twice the space and measure 20 to 24 feet. A driveway more than 40 feet long or one with curves should be at least 12 feet wide (14 feet is better). Curves in the driveway should have a minimum turning radius of 15 feet (measuring from the center of the half-circle to the circumference). The exception to the rule is when the flared part of the driveway meets the street. In this case, the radius can be 5 feet.

Circular drives can bring a stately appearance to the landscape, but they require a lot of space. For a full-size car to have room to turn, a 20-foot radius is best. If a circular drive has a parking area near

A circular drive is stately and makes moving through the property easy, but it requires a lot of space.

When a driveway works the way it should, an arriving visitor will drive directly to the parking space.

Perpendicular street side or curbside parking allows guests to pull in from the street. This works well on quiet streets but not on busy ones, because cars must back out into the street to exit.

the front door, the drive should be at least 16 feet wide to allow for passage around parked cars (see **Diagram 1** on page 31).

On a steep site, you may need to angle the drive across the property to maintain a safe grade. Driveways on steep slopes also need a level transition area of 12 feet or more where the drive meets the parking areas as well as where it meets the street.

An effective driveway design allows an arriving visitor to drive directly to a parking space without having to guess where to park. You can also use the layout of the driveway and the guest parking area to help determine which door your visitor will use to enter the house. "Lead" your guest to your home's entrance.

If your driveway leads directly to a garage or a carport, you may want to consider a turnaround, which will allow you to reverse directions and drive out forward rather than back into traffic. The turnaround can also serve as extra parking space.

Parking

When space allows, it's better to design parking on the lot instead of by the street. In many cases, parking simply means pulling into the driveway. However, you can create a variety of parking areas off the side of the driveway, from a parking court to a parallel parking space. These designs help if you have more than one car. If you are adding a family parking area, it should be close to the family entrance and convenient to the kitchen for carrying groceries. Consider secondary uses, too, such as a play area or basketball court.

The normal size of a typical parking space is 10 feet wide and 20 feet long. This is large enough to accommodate even the older, larger cars of yesterday. The number of parking spaces you plan for depends on the size and limitations of the lot plus your family's needs. Look to future needs, too, such as the space required for the cars of adult children. Also consider guest parking, especially if you live in a congested area.

Don't forget to provide turnaround space. This is especially important if you live on a busy street, where backing out of a driveway into heavy traffic can be dangerous. Plan for enough turnaround space so that a car can pull out into the street rather than backing out.

With curbside parking, the parking area is adjacent to the street. Cars can pull directly into the space, parking either parallel or perpendicular to the street. This is a good solution for small or steep lots. Parallel curbside parking requires 9 to 10 feet to allow cars to park and passengers to get out of the car safely. You need to allow 20 to 22 feet in length for each car (see **Diagram 2**). Spaces for perpendicular parking should be a minimum of 20 feet deep and 10 feet wide (see **Diagram 3**). Remember to allow for a wheel stop if there is a walkway along the parking area. This will keep the front end of the car from blocking the walkway. Perpendicular parking is easier on passengers getting in and out of the car, but it does require the driver to back into the street to leave. Another version of perpendicular parking is angled parking, which takes slightly less space. However, cars still must back out of the driveway (see **Diagram 4**).

Before planning curbside parking, check any local zoning restrictions or regulations. You will probably need a building permit.

The construction materials for driveways vary according to the expected use of the driveway and your budget. Asphalt, concrete, and gravel are often used and can easily accommodate most traffic.

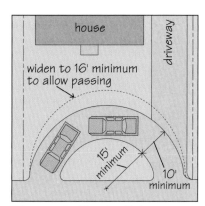

Diagram 1. *Circular Drive*

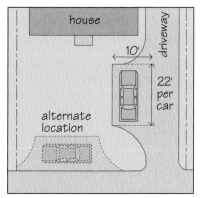

Diagram 2. *Parallel Parking*

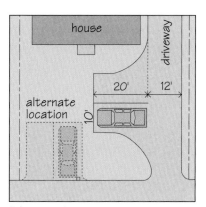

Diagram 3. *Perpendicular Parking*

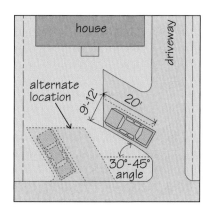

Diagram 4. *Angled Parking*

A walkway does more than lead guests to a front door. It delineates space, creating edges for a lawn or garden.

Walkways

Walkways are another area of the landscape that are often installed with little imagination or consideration of practicality. You can easily tell where a walkway ought to be by looking for footpaths worn through the yard. However, when deciding where to place a walkway in your landscape, be sure to consider more than just getting from point A to point B. Like driveways, the strong lines formed by walkways delineate space. They also help create planting beds and can organize your landscape into areas for different uses. Most walkways form a straight line from the street to the front door and tend to be too narrow.

A well-designed walkway guides people through your landscape efficiently and comfortably and is well defined. If your walkway is less than 40 feet long, avoid including unnecessary kinks or curves in its design. Make it as short or straight as possible. Curve or bend the walkway only when there is a reason. Although for walkways longer than 40 feet, a curve or an offset may be a welcome relief from the monotony of a straight line, a straight walkway is best for the primary access to guest parking. When the walkway is designed correctly, visitors can proceed from their car to the house without stepping on grass or dirt.

The width of a walkway will vary according to its intended use. A primary walkway, such as one leading to the front door, should be at least 42 inches wide, although 48 inches is better. This allows two people to walk comfortably side by side. A walkway in front of a large, expansive home should be even wider to keep it in proportion with the house. Seldom-used secondary walkways need only be 3 feet wide.

A gently curving walkway makes the journey from the street to the front door of this home just a little more appealing.

You can emphasize the lines of your walkways with bold plantings. Edging a walkway with thin strips of ground cover will make it look narrower. However, a band of ground cover or shrubs on both sides that measures at least twice the width of the walkway will make it appear wider.

A broad landing or small terrace at the head of the walkway will allow guests to gather comfortably when entering or exiting the house. It is also a nice spot for a bench or a visual element, such as a sculpture or a pot of flowers.

DIMENSIONS FOR STEPS

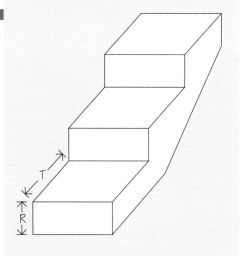

When planning for steps, follow this guideline: twice the riser (R) plus the tread (T) equals 26 inches (2R + T = 26"). This formula will help you figure out how many steps you need and what dimensions they should have. For example, if your riser is 6 inches, the tread should be 14 inches to equal 26 inches (2[6]+14=26).

Steps

Steps can make it easier to get to your car, to the mailbox, or to the street. If you have a flat site, you may want to create an elevation change to make the landscape more interesting. Steps double as places for children to sit and play or picnic. On large lots, you can use steps as spots to stop and look at the level below. On the other hand, avoid steps if accessibility is ever an issue.

First and foremost, steps must be safe and comfortable. Having the proper relationship between the treads (the part you step on) and the risers (the difference in elevation from one step to the next) will help ensure this. Generally, the shorter the riser is, the longer the tread should be. Treads less than 11 inches or risers less than 4 inches or greater than 7 inches are not recommended. See the box on this page to determine actual dimensions.

For steps to be functional, all steps in a series should be the same size. Each tread should be the same depth and each riser should be the same height. Avoid having one step by itself (it will be difficult to see), and be sure steps are properly lit. (See page 44 for more about lighting.)

Broad flagstone steps practically terrace this slope, making the ascent to the top of the garden easy and gradual. Railroad ties serve as risers.

Well-designed steps are a comfortable width and have the proper riser-to-tread ratio.

Patios and Decks

Planning a patio or deck is similar in some ways to planning an interior room. As an outdoor sitting or entertainment area, it is usually designed to be convenient to the living areas of the house and is often near the den or kitchen. Its shape is influenced by the architecture of the house, the location of utilities, the intended use, and the size and the contour of the yard. Patios must be built on the contour of the property, but a deck can be built over a slope or a difficult site. Existing trees are sometimes incorporated into the design of the patio or the deck; for example, holes can be cut through which they can grow.

Patios are best suited to level sites because they must be perfectly flat.

If you decide to build your deck around a tree, just make sure that the opening can be enlarged as the tree trunk widens.

The size of the patio or the deck depends on your needs and how many people will use it at a given time. If you are going to use your patio or deck for large groups, build it as large as possible. It also helps to know what kind of furniture you need to accommodate. If you plan to put a dining table and chairs and a glider on it, take these

HOW BIG SHOULD A PATIO OR A DECK BE?

If you plan to use a patio or a deck for entertaining, allow 25 square feet per person, with a minimum total size of 300 square feet.

When planning a deck, keep in mind the space requirements of patio furniture.

items into account as you design as well as any statuary or containers filled with plants.

In addition to their use in the backyard, patios and decks can serve as striking entryways in the front yard, creating a sense of welcome. They can also be inviting areas to receive your guests before bringing them into the house.

Quite often, very little planning is given to this space. It is not uncommon, especially with some older homes, to have a small landing or stoop outside the front door. Sometimes these miniporches barely accommodate two people. If you have an unattractive or impractical small paved entryway, you may need to dig it up and remove it, creating space for a new, larger one. A less expensive option would be to build a deck over the existing porch.

Optional Structures in the Landscape

After you have corrected any drainage or erosion problems, and after driveways, walkways, decks, and patios are planned, you need to look at some other landscape needs.

This ground-level wooden walkway also functions as an entry deck, giving residents a quiet place to sit.

Fences

Although fences are generally thought of as a way to separate your property from your neighbor's, they do a lot more than that. They can provide privacy, secure an area for children and pets, shield a garden from wind, define areas of your yard, or simply be an attractive landscaping feature. Although plants can accomplish many of the same tasks, fences don't have to grow into their role, and they offer architectural interest.

Fences can provide an attractive backdrop for plants, such as this pink azalea.

There are almost as many different kinds of fences as there are uses for them. Fences are classified as solid or open. Solid fencing provides the most privacy but may block summer breezes and sunlight. There is also the possibility, especially with tall, solid fences, of creating an imprisoning atmosphere. By contrast, some open fences, such as lattice, louver, and picket fences, provide a feeling of enclosure, while letting in breezes and sunlight.

A tall board fence provides instant privacy.

Regardless of the fence type or style you choose, check your local building codes for any restrictions before beginning to build. Often the height, the location, and even the materials used in a fence are regulated. A security fence should have a minimum height of 8 feet. For a privacy fence, you'll need a height of at least 6 feet. Often a fence is used simply to define part of a garden, whether it's an entryway or an herb garden. It can also serve as a backdrop for a flower border. Most fences like this are about 3 feet high. A picket fence is a popular choice, but you can create any style.

Sometimes a fence along a property line is owned and maintained by both neighbors. However, you can avoid the possibility of future problems by erecting a fence well within your property line. A split-rail fence is a purely decorative, open style that works well along property lines.

A chain-link fence is less expensive than other fences used to secure property. You can paint chain link a dark color, such as forest green or black, to help it blend with its surroundings. Or you can cover the fence with plants or vines.

TIPS FOR SCREENING

Screening items such as air-conditioning units from view while still providing access to them requires some creativity. The most common approach is to build a short wall or fence, plant dense shrubs, or use a combination of the two. Consider these factors:

• Height needed
• Direction from which the items are viewed
• Accessibility for servicing
• Direction of exhaust discharge (straight up or to the side)
• Air space around air-conditioning unit

To prevent the screen itself from becoming an eyesore, make it blend in with the surroundings. If you are installing a fence or a wall, use materials that were used in the building. If your house is painted, repeat those colors. If you use plants as a screen, match them to others in your yard. Be careful not to locate them where they'll get blasted by the unit's exhaust.

Walls

The main difference between a wall and a fence is permanence. They both serve similar functions of creating separation and providing privacy (except for retaining walls), but walls are enduring and may last as long as the house.

Walls for privacy and decoration. Wall designs vary greatly. They can be straight, stairstepped, angled, or serpentine. They can be solid or have an open design for some visibility and good air circulation. Always be sure that the style you choose blends with the house and other elements of the garden.

Walls are usually constructed from concrete, brick, adobe, rock, block, stone, or combinations of these. Block walls can be finished with paint or stucco.

Keep in mind that dark-colored walls tend to recede, while light or bright colors stand out. Use climbing plants or a landing in front of a long wall to help soften its broad expanse.

Because of their extreme weight, walls must often be built on *footings*. A footing is a below-grade foundation on which the wall sits. It's usually made from concrete and will prevent the wall from sinking deeper into the ground.

To build a freestanding masonry wall more than 3 feet tall, you may need a building permit. Check your local building codes.

Retaining wall. A retaining wall holds back soil on a sloping site. This type of wall is often used when terracing a site as it provides an effective way to create a level area on a steep slope.

Although the style of a retaining wall may be dictated by structural concerns, the finished wall can still be an attractive garden accent.

A brick privacy wall also makes an attractive background for this white azalea.

This short stone wall creates a separation between the house and street while providing a sense of enclosure along the path to the front door.

VINES FOR ARBORS

When choosing a vine for an arbor, consider how vigorously it grows. A wise selection will prevent maintenance problems later on. For example, wisteria will pull apart boards on all but the heaviest wooden arbors. On the other hand, yellow jessamine and Confederate jasmine are more delicate and have a trailing character that makes them better suited for home arbors.

Arbors, Pergolas, and Trellises

Overhead structures in your yard provide a ceiling for your outdoor room. They can be either freestanding or attached to your house. When well designed and properly sited, these structures provide an inviting, comfortable sitting or entertaining area. They can also serve as the focal point of a garden.

First, decide on the purpose of the structure. Some structures are open to the sky, giving a limited amount of protection from wind, sun, and rain. Others have a solid roof and do an effective job of shielding you from the elements. The principal function of some structures is to provide a support for vines.

The construction materials you use should suit the structure's function and the overall design of the landscape. If the structure is wood, build it from pressure-treated lumber or decay-resistant wood, such as cypress, redwood, or cedar. Or you may want to match the materials used in building your home.

Arbors. There are many styles of arbors, and the one you choose should be in harmony with the architecture of your house and the style of your garden. Whether classic or contemporary, an arbor can provide some shade and enclosure while linking different areas of the garden. Because there is no solid roof, arbors tend to provide dappled shade. Growing a vine on the arbor will create more shade and also screen wind. An arbor can provide almost instant shade, in comparison with the years it would take for a tree to provide the same cover. A deciduous vine will let some light in during the winter and provide deeper shade in summer.

A sturdy arbor is not only attractive but also provides an appropriate structure for growing vigorous vines.

Arbors with vines should be low enough to allow for pruning and other maintenance. Generally, a height of 8 to 10 feet is appropriate. Pressure-treated wood is the most common building material for arbors because it is easy to work with, blends well with the natural elements of a garden, and resists decay. You may finish your arbor with paint or stain; however, an arbor that is intended to support a vine will be easier to maintain if it is left to weather naturally.

Pergolas. A pergola is a tall overhead structure often used to provide cover for a walkway or a transition from one area to another, such as from a detached garage to a side door. It is usually made of columns supporting an overhead framework built of lumber.

Trellises. A trellis is a vertical framework that is often used for ornamental purposes or to create a barrier. A trellis acts as a screen, but because it is open, it never completely blocks light or a view. Most often, a trellis serves as an ornamental support for a vine. If you use it for this purpose, don't obscure the structure with a dense planting.

Important to the overall landscape scheme, this simple pergola serves as a covered entry from one portion of this garden to another.

A gazebo can be the focal point of a garden as well as a place to gather. Lighting will make it useful after dark.

Gazebos

Gazebos offer a sheltered outdoor setting for entertaining and relaxing and are often the central feature in a yard. They come in all different sizes and designs. Chippendale, contemporary, rustic, and open air are just a few of the choices available. Usually gazebos are freestanding and located away from the house. Sometimes, however, they are connected to a deck, a patio, or a fence, or they may be near the kitchen if they are used for entertaining.

The size of the gazebo depends on its intended use. If you plan to use it for entertaining, make it at least 10 feet in diameter. Plans sometimes call for built-in benches, but comfortable outdoor furniture that you can move around is often more practical. If you choose, you may equip your gazebo with a ceiling fan, a wet bar, a barbecue grill, lights, and stereo speakers. This will make it the hub of outdoor activity during good weather. Or, you may choose to create a small gazebo simply big enough to hang a hammock for a weekend nap.

Because gazebos are such attention-getters in the landscape, you should take care to site them properly. Their location and accessibility will determine how successful they are. Some factors to consider are nearness to traffic and neighbors, how it is seen from the house and yard, the direction of the sun and wind, and views from the gazebo.

Planters

Planters are raised planting beds generally built-in or adjacent to a structure, such as a deck, a patio, steps, a wall, or a fence. Planters create a low wall as well as provide a place to grow plants where there may not be much ground for planting.

There are several advantages to growing plants in planters. A big plus is drainage. Planters are usually built up off the ground, and, provided they have adequate weep holes, drain very well. They also show off and display any plant that is grown in them. And, because planters are often filled with potting soil, you are almost always assured of a good growing medium.

Another advantage of planters is that they elevate plants, making them easier to maintain. This is especially important if you are growing anything that requires a lot of attention. If you build your own planter, include an edge wide enough sit on. This will give you a place to sit while tending the plants.

Planters decorate an attractive sitting area in the garden.

TIP FOR PLANTERS

The soil in planters tends to dry out quickly. To combat this, choose a high-quality potting soil that retains moisture. It also helps to add mulch and locate the planter where it doesn't receive full sun all day.

Tall planters, such as this one, make gardening with flowers, herbs, or vegetables easier because you don't have to bend over to maintain them.

Play Structures

Having a safe, inviting, and fun area for children to play not only is great for children but also provides peace of mind for adults. Play spaces require planning and a design that suits the needs, ages, and interests of the children and the limitations of the property. Locate a play area where adults can see it from the house.

Play equipment ranges from a playhouse to a simple swing hung from a backyard tree limb to a custom-designed climbing apparatus costing thousands of dollars. Keep in mind the space needed for each piece of equipment. Tetherballs and swings, for example, need more clearance than slides or seesaws. Also, be aware of hidden dangers, such as exposed nut-and-bolt heads, rough edges, and splinters.

A well-planned play area should be flexible in its design and layout. Not only will children's interest in play equipment evolve over time, but eventually, the equipment will be abandoned. After the kids leave home, what do middle-aged adults do with two swings and a slide? With foresight and creativity, you can transform that old play area into an intimate garden space.

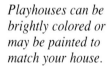

Playhouses can be brightly colored or may be painted to match your house.

This garden pond is the central feature of the garden.

Garden Ponds

There is a place in almost every landscape for the magic of water. Because a garden pond or pool has such an obvious presence in a yard, its location is important. Different factors influence its placement. Will it be seen both from inside the house and from the yard? Do you plan to have water plants? Do you want to stock it with fish or attract birds and other wildlife? If you are growing water lilies or other flowering aquatics, your pond needs to get at least six hours of sunlight a day. Fish will need water at least 18 inches deep.

Three categories of garden pond design are formal, informal, and natural.

Formal ponds or pools are usually geometric and tend to be symmetrically shaped. Fountains and sculptures are often used as accessories.

Informal ponds or pools may be made from containers not traditionally associated with ponds. Barrels, washtubs, and tanks are examples of receptacles used to create a self-contained water feature.

Natural ponds or pools should not appear man-made. For the most natural appearance, locate the pond in a low area of the yard, since that's where ponds are found in nature.

A pond must fit into the overall design of the yard. Otherwise, it will appear out of place and seem like an afterthought.

Hardly a pond by definition, this small fountain created in a large concrete pot brings the sound of water into a garden easily and inexpensively.

HIDE THE LIGHT
SOURCE

The biggest mistake people often make when installing night lighting is to locate the lightbulb incorrectly. Regardless of the effect you want or the fixture you use, remember never to let the source of the illumination be seen. You should be able to enjoy the results and effects of the lighting without looking directly into the bulb.

Outdoor Lighting

For many, the setting of the sun and the onset of darkness mean the end of another day in the garden. But with outdoor lighting, you can extend the length of time you enjoy your garden with the flick of a switch. At night, the landscape wears a different face in the glow of night lighting.

The four major reasons people use outdoor lighting are aesthetics, security, safety, and recreation or entertaining. As with other garden design projects, planning is the key to good outdoor lighting. With proper planning, you can solve more than one of your lighting needs at the same time. For example, the fixture that illuminates an accent tree may also shed light on nearby steps.

When designing a lighting scheme, refer to the working drawings discussed earlier in this book. Indicate on the map the areas you want to illuminate, and then use different-colored pencils for each use. All garden designers are not experts in lighting, so if you need help, do your homework. In some large cities, you may be able to find design firms that specialize exclusively in landscape lighting.

Aesthetics

By lighting only certain areas or elements in your garden, you control how visitors perceive or view your yard at night. To be successful, planning and experimenting are crucial. Before you buy your first lightbulb, decide what results you want from your lighting. There are a variety of different light fixtures available, each one creating its own effects. Here are some of the more popular ones.

Accent lights are small fixtures placed close to the ground. They provide a subtle source of decorative lighting almost anywhere in the garden.

Floodlights have a broad light beam that covers large areas. They can create dramatic silhouettes or be installed on the ground and aimed skyward to uplight trees.

Mushroom lights are fixtures that measure at least 1 foot tall. They project light downward and are often used to illuminate pathways and steps.

Spotlights have a narrow or focused beam. They are commonly used to illuminate a specific area or an individual plant or garden feature.

Well lights are installed in the ground. They are usually flush at ground level and are used for uplighting.

To get an idea of how lighting will affect your landscape, experiment at dusk with a large flashlight or a portable electric light and an extension cord. Place your portable light source in different locations in your yard and see how it looks. Notice the effects you get by aiming the beam in different directions and by varying the height off the ground. Be careful not to shine the light into your neighbor's yard or house. Some lighting effects that you can create include these.

Accent lighting accentuates specific landscape features. Spotlighting, for example, can focus attention on individual plants or statuary. You can create striking effects by washing light across a textured surface, such as a wall, a fence, or a chimney.

Backlighting illuminates walls, fences, tree trunks, or other large, vertical objects (see **Diagram 1** on page 46).

Diffused lighting uses translucent screens to soften and mute harsh light. This lighting is often used above decks and patios.

Downlighting mimics natural light. The fixture is located

Uplighting highlights the multiple trunks of this small tree.

Diagram 1. *Backlighting*

Diagram 2. *Downlighting*

Diagram 3. *Uplighting*

overhead with the light shining down from above. When used in trees or on high poles or buildings, the light produces a broad, moonlight effect (see **Diagram 2**).

Mirror lighting is used to light subjects that you want reflected in a garden pool or pond.

Moonlighting uses floodlights in trees to shine down through the tree limbs, creating a filigree of limb shadows on the ground.

Shadowing generally involves aiming a light that is set near the ground at a specific object, such as a craggy shrub. A light used in this way will cast an interesting shadow on a wall or another surface behind it.

Uplighting projects a beam upward, often into tree branches and foliage. The fixtures are usually located at ground level but can also be installed in a tree canopy (see **Diagram 3**).

Security

Outdoor lighting brightens dark corners, illuminates heavily planted locations, and casts light on entry and arrival areas. The type of security light you use depends on the area you want illuminated. Choices range from a small low-wattage fixture that lights up a limited space to a floodlight that blankets the entire yard. You may use floodlights to illuminate dark areas around windows and doors by backlighting and uplighting.

Here are the four most common mechanisms for controlling outdoor security lights.

Manual wall switches. These light switches are similar to those in your home.

Motion detectors. These devices are sensitive to moving objects and will turn lights on if they sense motion.

Photoelectric cells. These mechanisms are sensitive to daylight and automatically turn lights on at dusk and off at dawn.

Timer switches. Timer switches turn fixtures on and off at preset times.

SECURITY LIGHTING

If your front door opens outward and you use only one porch light, install the fixture on the same side of the wall as the door handle. This allows you to see your visitors clearly and keeps them out of the shadow of the opened door.

Safety

Without adequate lighting, moving safely in and around your property can be a challenge. Obstacles such as steps, low tree branches, and garden paths that are easily seen in daylight become invisible at night. Good night lighting allows you to navigate the yard safely.

Recreation and Entertaining

When an outdoor entertainment area is properly lit, the people using it are unaware of the lighting. Fixtures usually are located overhead or installed under railings or steps. Keep in mind that you need to properly light access to and from the recreation and entertaining area.

Lighting Systems

After you have designed your outdoor lighting scheme, including where to place your fixtures and how to turn them on and off, you must decide which lighting system to use. Your two major choices are 120-volt or 12-volt (low-voltage) systems. Each has advantages and disadvantages.

120-volt system. This system utilizes electricity at the same voltage as the lights in your house. It is the best choice if you need bright light. If you have an existing wiring system, you may want to hire an electrician to add this new system.

Low-voltage, 12-volt system. These systems are custom-made for the do-it-yourselfer. They are inexpensive to buy and easy to install and operate. There are rarely any code restrictions, so hiring an electrician is usually unnecessary. The key to the system is a small plug-in transformer or power pack. It reduces the 120 volts from your house circuit to a nondangerous 12 volts. A two-wire cable runs from the transformer, along or under the ground, attaching fixtures along the way. The size of the transformer determines how many fixtures you can use. Also, remember the longer the length of the wire, the dimmer the light.

PLACES FOR SAFETY LIGHTING

Doorways
Driveway entrance
Guest parking area
Sidewalks and paths
Stairs and steps
Turnaround space

Dramatic lighting brings this pool area to life at night.

Planting Design

Planting design—that is, deciding what plants to use where—is the final step in designing a landscape plan.

The simple alignment of these crepe myrtles enhances the eye appeal of the house.

When you drive through a neighborhood, you always come across some landscaped yards that stand out. The trees, shrubs, lawns, and flowers of these yards work together so that the end result is beautiful, inspiring, and functional.

Although landscaping projects can include everything from decks and driveways to daffodils, most people usually think plants when they think landscaping. How you select plants and how you place them for visual interest (as well as for practical solutions) will make the difference between a hodge-podge planting and one that makes a statement.

Visual Concepts of Planting Design

To learn how to place plants correctly in a landscape, you will want to review the basic theories of design. Although this may seem irrelevant, design concepts are essential tools when you want an exceptional landscape. A good grasp of the principles of design can go a long way toward creating a professional-looking landscape.

Line. Line is one of the most important and most visible design elements. It leads the eye to a desired destination. In the landscape, lines are created by driveways, walkways, paths, patio edges, planting beds, edgings, and fences.

Lines also evoke different responses. For example, a vertical line leading away from you seems to draw you forward, while a horizontal line is more relaxing and tends to slow you down. Flowing lines are more relaxing than straight ones. In landscape design, straight lines are used to develop formality, whereas curving lines are more typical of informal plantings.

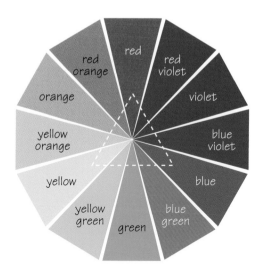

The color wheel can be useful in determining what colors are compatible.

Color. Color is the most noticeable landscape element. Because our eyes are naturally drawn to color, it is important to use it carefully.

The color wheel on this page shows how colors work together. It lets you preview various color combinations and simplifies color selection. To use the color wheel, cut a small equilateral triangle of paper, and position it on the wheel so that its points are on the three primary colors—red, yellow, and blue. As you rotate the triangle, the points will rest on trios that work well together, making it easy for you to group flowers of corresponding colors. But remember that green is your major background color when grouping plants.

This Japanese maple provides vivid color to the fall landscape.

Form. Very simply, form is the shape of the plant. These shapes add interest to a garden design. Different forms serve different purposes. (See pages 57 and 60 for more about forms of trees and shrubs.)

Mass. Masses of plants form the body of a landscape design, providing boundaries and separating one area from another. A mass of shrubs, such as a hedge, can create a screen. The same mass will serve as a boundary, giving shape and definition to the open area, often a lawn, beside it. Balancing masses of plants with open areas provides a garden with grace and form.

Texture. The texture of plants is divided into three categories: fine, medium, and coarse. You can create an exciting landscape composition by mixing plants of different textures. Sometimes textural

In this grouping of tropical plants, contrasts in texture can be just as dramatic as combinations of color.

contrast in a garden is even more effective than contrasts in color. (See page 55 for more about using texture as a design tool.)

Design Functions of Plants

There are many things to consider when choosing plants for your landscape design. Every house is unique, and plantings can be arranged to suit the style of each house. You can dramatically change the appearance of a house and a garage, as well as an entire yard, with plants. Keep in mind that you will choose plants not only to provide beauty but also to perform a variety of functions.

A planting design should frame the house and define spaces, giving an overall outline to the landscape. Plants can also screen views and create privacy and a sense of enclosure. As a bonus, some plants have a pleasing fragrance as well as seasonal color and beauty. This chapter and the next will show you how design and plant selection combine to create a landscape worthy of your home.

Foundation Plantings

When you select plants, keep in mind that the house will always be the center of attention. Plants should complement a home, not compete with it. In most neighborhoods, it is common to see a line of shrubs straight across the front of a house and down the sides. Often plants cover as much as two-thirds of the structure. From a distance, this poor design creates the illusion of a house sitting on a green pillow of shrubbery. Use plantings of shrubs and trees to frame outstanding parts of the home, not to hide them.

Shrubs work well at the outside corners of a house, and because of their size, trees look especially good beyond the corners. When planting trees and shrubs, give careful thought to their placement in the yard. Their location depends on the angle at which the house will be viewed. A home is rarely seen from a direct, straight-on perspective. Most of the time, passersby see it from an angle. Take this into consideration when locating foundation plants.

Professionals often use the front door as a focal point when designing front-yard landscapes. Because the door is the focus of the house, plantings should draw attention to it. Accent plants are purposely used to highlight or emphasize the front entrance. Lighting fixtures, brass hardware, decorative glass, and contrasting door paint can also accent a front entrance.

This house was plain and uninviting before the foundation planting and the approach to the house were relandscaped.

A new walkway and foundation plants, carefully selected for their color, texture, and form, create an inviting approach to the front door.

Screening and Enclosure

Plants not only provide beauty, but they also do an excellent job of screening undesirable views. They can attractively enclose an area to provide privacy and can even block wind. Some of the more successful landscapes are those in which trees and shrubs have been used to create spaces rather than fill them up. When properly planned, these enclosures or outdoor rooms can provide a feeling of safety and security.

Consider these factors when choosing trees and shrubs for screening and enclosure.

Evergreen plants that branch all the way to the ground provide excellent screening and year-round privacy.

Evergreen or deciduous. If you need a year-round screen, use evergreen trees and shrubs. The bare branches of most deciduous plants provide little in the way of screening. However, these plants can be a good source of seasonal interest when they are used with evergreens for contrast.

Plant height. How tall should your enclosure be? First determine the height requirements of your screen, and then choose the appropriate plants. Installing shrubs that grow only 5 feet tall will do little to screen a two-story building behind your backyard.

Lower branches. For your screen to be effective and your enclosure to be complete, the branches of the plants should extend to the ground. Some trees and shrubs lose their lower branches as they mature, while others retain them.

Evergreen trees that retain their lower branches include Canadian hemlock, Leyland cypress, and Southern magnolia.

Evergreen shrubs that retain their lower branches include some azaleas, Burford holly, camellias, Japanese cleyera, and Nellie R. Stevens holly.

TIPS FOR FOUNDATION PLANTINGS

• Make a narrow house appear wider by using low plantings at a uniform height. If space permits, expand plant beds at the far corners of the house to create a feeling of width. Avoid using tall, slender plants. They can create a disjointed effect, making a house appear smaller.
• Make a tall, boxlike home appear less imposing by using large, massive trees as both a frame and a backdrop. Use fences, walls, or plantings to lengthen the home visually at each end.
• Complement long, low-roofed houses by using dwarf plants and spreading plants. Try not to let shrubs reach the roof overhang or cover windows.

Masonry edging gives a crisp, finished look to a garden.

Bed Lines and Edging

Bed lines, or the outlines of a planting bed that define its shape, can often mean the difference between a nice landscape and an outstanding one. These edges separate plant beds from lawns and from other plant beds with crisp lines. They can be curved, straight, or a combination of the two, depending on the desired effect. Straight lines generally create a more formal look than curved lines. If you want a curved bed, avoid weak or erratic lines. Bold, sweeping bed lines are stronger.

After you lay out your bed lines, you need to think about the edging. Edging neatly defines a plant bed, giving it a definite outline and setting it off from the rest of the yard. The benefits are both decorative and practical.

Edging can help contain beds of ground cover as well as prevent weeds and grasses from encroaching on plant beds. Lay your edging material flush with the ground to make mowing easier. The edging acts as a track for the lawnmower wheels, permitting a neat, clean cut of the grass next to the bed.

Design Techniques

Keep in mind that the tree or shrub you plant now will not be the same size at maturity. If a plant looks sparse at first, just remember that a good landscape looks better several years after it is planted than it does when first installed.

Choose Plants That Fit the Space

Select a plant that has the same shape and size as the space it will fill. For example, low-growing or spreading plants, such as ground cover junipers, are best suited for restricted spaces. These plants rarely, if ever, need pruning and therefore work well under low windows or in front of short porches. Upright plants, such as Japanese cleyera, are commonly used in tight corners or vertical spaces. With the variety of shrubs available in each category, there is no reason to "force" a plant into a space where it doesn't fit.

Sometimes it is difficult to look at a foot-tall plant in a nursery container and imagine how large it will grow. Ask your nurseryman about the mature size or refer to Plant Profiles beginning on page 68 for information on commonly used plants.

Cluster several plants of the same type to give each plant group a strong presence.

Cluster Plants

Although no two sites are the same, certain design techniques such as clustering can be effective in most any landscape. Cluster plants (predominately shrubs) at corners and at other variations in the building's facade. Any place there is a recess or a protrusion is a potential spot to group plants. You might cluster plants where the garage joins the house or where the front porch is attached.

These groupings are then connected or visually tied together; often lower-growing groups of plants, such as masses of dwarf shrubs or ground cover, do the job. This low band of plants helps unify the composition and makes the entire planting design look finished without hiding the house.

Mass Plants for Impact

In addition to small clusters or single specimens, you may want to group large numbers of plants, especially small plants, such as ground covers or dwarf yaupon hollies, to form a large mass or drift of plants. This swath of uniform color or texture spreading over a large area makes an impact, especially when viewed from a distance.

Limit the Number of Plant Types

Avoid using too many different kinds of plants in your design. The variety of shrubs and trees you choose will greatly affect the success of your landscape. Too many contrasting plants can result in a jumbled horticultural "zoo." You can add to the unity and rhythm of your landscape by using masses of a reasonable number of species, along with a few clusters or single plants for accent.

CLUSTER AN ODD NUMBER

When clustering plants, use an odd number, if possible. Clusters of three, five, or seven plants are visually more pleasing than even-number groupings.

Limiting the types of landscape plants and planting them in clusters or masses produces a simple, uncluttered design.

On the other hand, a lack of variety can be monotonous. Using only one or two types of plants can be boring. As a general rule, limit your design to several plant types that are repeated throughout the design. Then add accent plants to keep the design from becoming monotonous. If your house and property are exceptionally large, adjust the rule accordingly.

Factors Influencing Use of Plants

Plants decorate a landscape just as paint and furnishings decorate a house. But unlike paint, wallpaper, or furniture, plants change over the seasons. Because they are living things, you will need to study carefully the characteristics of the plants you choose for your landscape design. Below are four factors to consider.

Rate of Growth

Your choice of plants will be influenced by how quickly you want a planting to fill in. Generally, you should allow a planting at least two years to begin looking settled and "grown in."

Don't be tempted by trees that grow rapidly, such as red maple. Disease, weak wood, insects, and other problems make many fast-growing plants, especially trees, undesirable. However, many ground covers and shrubs that are relatively fast growing are reliable.

Keep in mind that vigorously growing shrubs will require frequent pruning if you place them in a location that doesn't suit their size. In contrast, slow-growing plants require much less attention to keep them at a desirable size or shape. Some slow-growing, low shrubs, such as Rotunda holly and dwarf Indian hawthorn, never grow taller than a few feet.

Plant Shape

Plants, like people, come in all shapes and sizes. Their shape or profile is called their growth habit. If left to grow undisturbed, some plants will eventually become tall and thin, while others will be short and round. Trees and shrubs are classified in many categories of plant shapes. (See pages 57 and 60 for some of these.)

Plants function in many ways in a design. These crepe myrtles and boxwoods provide a sense of enclosure.

Plant Texture

Every plant has a visual texture classified as either fine, medium, or coarse. Its texture is determined by the size, shape, and arrangement of the leaves on the plant. Always include at least one plant from each category in your plant composition. Juxtaposing different textures adds visual interest to your landscape.

A coarse-textured plant is one with large foliage. These plants may also have thorns, spikes, or leaves with stickers, points, or jagged edges. Japanese aucuba, loquat, and Southern magnolia are good examples.

Fine-textured plants give the illusion of being lacy and open. They have a light, wispy character. Examples of fine-textured plants include boxwood, juniper, and most ornamental grasses.

The leaves of medium-textured plants are neither overly large nor small and delicate. While the majority of plants fall into this category, some of the most popular ones are forsythia, ginkgo, Japanese cleyera, river birch, and sasanqua camellia.

Plant Color

The colorful blooms of a plant are usually more enticing than its leaves, stems, or bark. Because of this, it is easy to overlook what color these may turn throughout the seasons. If you fail to pay attention to all the color aspects of your plants, you can end up with an unattractive combination.

A red Japanese maple is the star in this dynamic composition of various plant textures, colors, and forms.

Whenever possible, mass plants of the same color, foliage, or bloom. This creates a greater impact than a sprinkling of different colors. By massing color you can avoid "shotgun design"— random placement of plants growing helter-skelter in the landscape. And remember not to overdo it. Some of the more successful landscapes feature color only as an accent.

Keep in mind that color draws attention wherever it is used. Don't attempt to hide or disguise eyesores with colorful plants; the color will attract attention to the problem.

Although color is an important element in planting design, don't make it the primary emphasis. Form, texture, and healthy foliage are more lasting qualities in landscape design.

Choosing Trees and Shrubs for Design

Large trees can set the tone and mood for an entire landscape. Whenever large, healthy trees exist in a landscape, chances are you will want to keep them.

The varied sizes and shapes of plants, along with their textures and colors, will create a beautiful outdoor room.

After determining all the structural elements of a landscape, a landscape designer then begins to choose plants. Whatever effects you want to achieve in planting design—textural contrast, color, an interesting foundation planting, privacy—require an understanding of the plants themselves. You will select trees and shrubs as you begin the final phase of your landscape. Your last decision will be to choose flowers for your landscape.

Trees in the Landscape

Trees, more than any other garden ingredient, define a property. They are the difference between an open lot and a forested retreat. Their influence on people's lives and people's reverence for them have been documented in songs, stories, poems, pictures, and sculptures.

Trees also provide both practical and aesthetic benefits. When you are looking for that perfect tree, do some homework. First consider what it will be used for—then select a tree whose form is suited to its use.

Columnar

Irregular

Form

A tree's shape or form (also called profile or silhouette) is one of its most obvious features. You will want to choose a tree with a form that best fits your site.

Columnar. These trees have a strong, upright shape and can sometimes be a landscaping challenge. They can look like an exclamation point. Columnar trees, such as Leyland cypress, can be effective silhouetted against buildings or walls or planted as shoulder-to-shoulder screens.

Irregular. Some trees appear to have no definite shape. Their growth habit seems random, with branches growing in all directions. A young ginkgo is a typical example.

Oval or rounded. Some of the most popular shade trees have this form. American beech, sugar maple, and willow oak are a few of the many oval-shaped trees.

Pyramidal. The silhouettes of these trees resemble the traditional Christmas tree. They have a strong visual presence in the landscape and should be used carefully, perhaps as an accent. Canadian hemlock and Foster holly have a pyramidal form.

Spreading. If it is possible for a tree to be regal, such a tree would have a spreading form. A good example is the live oak, with its majestic, stately branches reaching out wider than the tree is high.

Vase shaped. This form is the opposite of the pyramidal shape. It is wide at the top and narrow at the bottom. Winged euonymus is a popular treelike shrub with vase-type branching. American elm and Japanese zelkova are classic vase-shaped trees.

Weeping. This form has a soft, graceful appearance. Because their drooping foliage attracts attention, these pendulous trees make good garden accents or specimens. Weeping cherry and weeping willow are popular examples.

Oval or rounded

Pyramidal

Spreading

Vase shaped

Weeping

Shade

Although trees provide many practical benefits, none is more appreciated than the cooling effect of shade. The presence or absence of shade may also govern what will grow beneath a tree. The amount of shade a tree provides is influenced by these factors.

Deciduous or evergreen. Deciduous trees, such as maple and hickory, provide the deepest shade during the summer at midday. Needle-leafed trees, such as pines, cast a dappled shade. Broad-leafed evergreen trees, such as Southern magnolia and dense, needle-leafed trees, such as hemlock, produce a heavy shade that makes it difficult to grow anything beneath them.

Location. A tree's location in the yard will affect what gets shaded and what doesn't. Remember that the sun rises in the East and sets in the West. Before randomly planting a tree, investigate what the best location would be for maximum shade benefits. Shade trees located on the south side and on the west side of the house provide the most protection from afternoon heat in summer.

Tree size and shape. Tall, skinny trees or short, wide ones may be beautiful to look at, but they usually don't provide the best shade. Tall trees that have a rounded or spreading form are generally the best sources of seasonal shade. Another factor that affects the degree of shade a tree provides is the height of its branches. Most of the time, tall trees whose lower limbs are high overhead allow sunlight to filter through their branches.

Flowering crepe myrtle trees brighten the landscape in summer.

Color

If you choose the right combination of trees, it is possible to have year-round color in your garden. Some trees sport a different color for each season.

While evergreen trees give constant color, deciduous trees begin to display their new foliage in the spring. Many of them, such as dogwood and most fruit trees, have dazzling flowers.

By the time summer arrives, these trees are cloaked in foliage. The leaves not only come in different shades of green but also scarlet to deep purple. Another source of excellent summer color is crepe myrtle; this tree is available in many selections that offer an array of outstanding summer blooms.

When the crisp air of autumn arrives, so does a change of color. Deciduous trees that just a couple months earlier were covered in green turn to a blaze of yellow, scarlet, orange, or red. A tree's fruit can add even more color. The red and orange berries of dogwood and hawthorn brighten the landscape and are a favorite of birds.

Winter has its own beauty. When deciduous trees shed their leaves, their bark and structure take on more prominence. The gray and brown tree trunks provide a muted contrast to nearby evergreens. Some evergreens may even retain their berries into winter.

Height and Spread

Because trees are usually long-term investments, you should select them with care. If you take the time to find out how tall and wide a tree will grow, you can avoid future problems. If you plant a tall-growing tree under low power lines or a spreading tree too close to a building or sidewalk, problems may develop later.

Consider a tree's root system, too. When large trees are used near a septic drain field, their roots can clog the system. Some tree's roots can also buckle driveways and sidewalks if planted too close, especially if the soil is heavy clay.

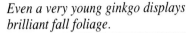

Even a very young ginkgo displays brilliant fall foliage.

These oak trees, valued for their intense fall color, provide deep shade in the summer.

59

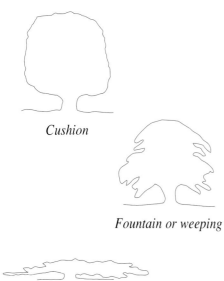

Cushion

Fountain or weeping

Matting

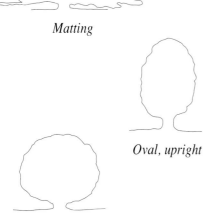

Oval, upright

Rounded or mounding

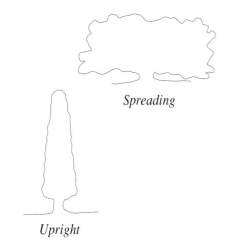

Spreading

Upright

Shrubs in the Landscape

For some people, shrubs are plants used around the foundation of a house. For others, they are pruned hedges that sometimes form a visual boundary between properties. For still others, shrubs are a source of seasonal color, fruit, or fresh holiday greenery.

Shrubs are all of these things and more. They are the backbone of a landscape design, working to create walls of foliage, ornamentation, and even ground cover in a garden.

The Size and Shape of Shrubs

As shrubs mature, they not only grow larger, but they also develop a distinct shape or silhouette. When choosing plants for your landscape, select shrubs that have a shape that fits the space they will fill. Most shrubs can be classified into one of the following seven categories:

Cushion. A soft, compact shape defines these shrubs. Their foliage is usually dense, and they have a neat appearance. Examples include dwarf yaupon holly and Heller Japanese holly.

Fountain or weeping. This graceful form, which includes forsythia and Reeves spirea, is often used in masses to create a striking effect or as a specimen plant.

Matting. The low-growing, ground-hugging shrubs in this category make excellent ground covers. Some, such as cotoneaster and creeping juniper, carpet the landscape and are often used on hillsides or as a substitute for grass.

Oval, upright. The shrubs in this category are taller than they are wide. They are great for screening and for creating spaces and enclosures. Examples include camellia, dwarf Burford holly, Japanese cleyera, and wax myrtle.

Rounded or mounding. These versatile plants are as wide as they are tall. They make good foundation plants and hedges as they work well in masses. Dwarf boxwood and Indian hawthorn are two shrubs with this silhouette.

Spreading. Shrubs with a spreading form grow horizontally and are wider than they are tall. Examples include barberry and cotoneaster.

Upright. Plants with this vertical shape are most commonly used as accents. Examples include Japanese cleyera and leatherleaf mahonia.

This planting weaves a dramatic tapestry of shrub forms and textures. It includes a tree-form waxleaf privet, a ground cover of creeping juniper, an upright juniper, and the rosettes of sago palms.

Uses for Shrubs

The uses for shrubs are as varied as the spaces they fill. A few of their more popular functions are as foundation plantings, as windbreaks, or as privacy screens.

Foundation Plantings

As you read in the previous chapter, shrubs are often planted at the foundation of a home. They soften the transition between the vertical walls of the house and the horizontal ground. Avoid the common mistake of planting shrubs in straight rows in front and down the sides of a house. Instead, group shrubs at the corners of a house and at other structural breaks in the facade.

This simple foundation planting includes clusters of shrubs that frame portions of the house.

Windbreaks

Strong winds can be deflected by using tall, dense shrubs, such as Burford holly. Any shrub used as a year-round windbreak should be evergreen, and its branches should extend to the ground. Shrubs come in all heights and widths, so determine what size your windbreak needs to be, and then choose the appropriate plant.

Controlling Circulation

Strategically placed shrubs can influence where people walk. A grouping of plants at the intersection of two sidewalks can prevent people from "cutting corners." You can even use shrubs with thorns or stickers, such as barberry, leatherleaf mahonia, or Rotunda holly, to help reroute foot traffic. Shrubs are also used to emphasize an entrance or to define a driveway or a sidewalk.

Screening and Enclosure

With the proper shrubs, you can grow "walls" to screen views or to enclose a section of your yard. The desired height of your screen and the available space dictates which shrubs you use. Choose evergreen plants that retain their lower limbs, if you want total enclosure and year-round privacy. Some good shrubs for screening include camellia, dwarf Burford holly, and Japanese cleyera.

Backdrop

Evergreen shrubs in particular are good backdrops for other plants. An evergreen wall looks great behind a large flowerbed, but you can also use it as a backdrop for a specimen flowering shrub or even a garden sculpture.

These dwarf Burford hollies will eventually form a dense screen that hides the utility box and creates a sense of separation from the yard next door.

Color

Shrubs are often overlooked as a source of garden color. A shrub's flowers, fruit, and foliage can provide continual landscape interest month after month. There are flowering shrubs for every season. Deciduous as well as evergreen shrubs can provide a palette of different colors for your garden. The box on page 63 lists shrubs that provide color throughout the seasons.

Many shrubs, such as this azalea, will contribute color to your design. When choosing a shrub for a specific use, be sure to consider its color and season of bloom.

SHRUB COLOR FOR EVERY SEASON

The flowers, foliage, and berries of these plants will provide year-round color for your garden.

Spring: azalea, flowering quince, forsythia, Japanese kerria, spirea
Summer: glossy abelia, oakleaf hydrangea, oleander, Rose-of-Sharon
Fall: chokeberry, oakleaf hydrangea, sasanqua camellia, winged euonymus
Winter: Burford holly, common camellia, nandina

ANNUALS AND PERENNIALS FOR COLOR

Annual and perennial flowers in the landscape are like ornaments on a Christmas tree. They are the finishing touch. An attractive flowerbed catches the eye of passersby.

Be sure to give careful thought to the location of your flowerbeds. Many people plant annuals and perennials without considering how they will relate to the overall design of the landscape.

Keep in mind that color in the landscape is seasonal. The entire layout of the landscape should not hinge on flowers. Instead, the design and the composition of the yard should stand on their own. Reserve color as an accent.

Red caladiums add a touch of summer color to this garden.

Lawns in the Landscape

Design your lawn so that it has a definite shape and clearly defined edges.

A well-designed lawn should flow smoothly around the house.

The location and layout of your lawn should be one of the first things you consider. Most people know where they want grass. But getting the lawn to look like a green carpet is a challenge.

One of the major factors that makes the difference between a beautiful lawn and an average one is shape. The first step in planning your lawn is to define its exact shape or layout. The next time you see an ideal lawn on the cover of a magazine or in the neighborhood, look at its edges. Chances are that the grass stops at the bed line. It doesn't wander among the shrubs or disappear into the flowers.

How you will use your lawn and how much time you have to maintain it will help determine its size, shape, and location. Some folks think of a lawn only as an area for displaying the house and showcasing the plants. It may never be walked on except to maintain it.

For other families, the lawn is an extension of the living room or den. It is a place for entertaining, playing badminton, running through sprinklers, or just relaxing in a lawn chair.

After deciding how you will use your lawn, look for elements in the yard that might present problems.

Slopes. The more level the yard, the easier it is to maintain a lawn. Steep hillsides or uneven lots can make mowing difficult and can even be dangerous. A good alternative to grass is a ground cover that doesn't need mowing. Hardy ground covers that love sun and do well on slopes include ajuga, cotoneaster, daylilies, Japanese star jasmine, and spreading junipers.

Trees. You will have many obstacles to overcome if you try to grow grass under trees. Most grass does best in sun; in fact, the more sun the better. The shade of a tree creates a less than desirable growing environment for a healthy lawn. To allow sunlight to penetrate a tree canopy, some homeowners selectively prune and thin it. This increases the odds of the grass doing well. Grass growing under a tree has to compete with the tree for the limited amount of nutrients and moisture in the soil, with the tree usually winning.

Some trees, especially older ones, have exposed roots. These roots make it extremely difficult to mow any grass that may have grown beneath it. Adding dirt to the area won't solve the problem. Using topsoil to cover the roots will only provide temporary relief, because the roots will eventually be exposed again. This space beneath the tree then becomes an area that lends itself to using ground cover instead of grass. Shade-tolerant plants, such as ivy, liriope, pachysandra, and periwinkle, do well in areas where grass won't grow. And once the ground cover is established, no mowing is needed.

Using ground cover instead of grass not only makes life simpler, but these plants also add texture to the landscape. You can create striking results by using beds of coarse-textured ground cover next to a carpetlike mowed lawn.

Existing elements. Plant beds, structures, streams, rock outcroppings, ponds, and other permanent structures define much of the landscape and will limit where you locate your lawn. But don't treat each element independently. Use a meandering lawn to unify and pull together the different "ingredients" of your landscape.

Growing grass in heavy shade is difficult. In this unique design, just a ribbon of grass is used to unify the entire landscape.

EDGE YOUR LAWN

Use an edging next to plant beds, natural areas, and shrubs to contain the grass and to give the lawn definition. Some of the more popular edgings include brick, cobblestone, treated wood, poured concrete, rocks, strips of metal or plastic, and plantings of liriope. An edging may also simply be a clean-lined trench filled with mulch.

65

Landscape Makeover

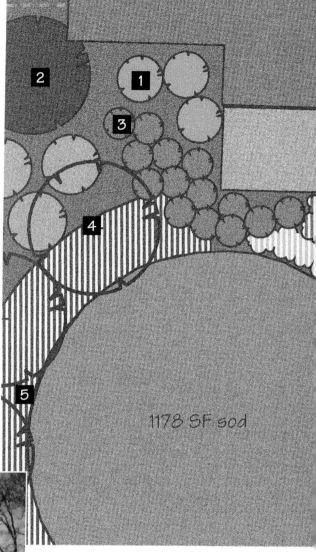

The success of any planting design is measured by how well it ties a house and site together.

In preparation for a landscape makeover, the front yard of this new house was photographed and then carefully assessed. A computerized drawing depicts the finished, mature planting. The image gives you an idea of the effect a good planting plan has on a landscape.

The site had few existing factors restricting the overall design. A young tree, the only significant plant in the front yard, was left in place and will eventually grow taller than the house. Two short brick columns at the front of the walkway were removed, because they served no purpose and detracted from the house.

1178 SF sod

Before

After

Follow the numbers on the plan above to see the suggestions for plant combinations that will produce a pleasing design. The computer-generated final result is pictured at left.

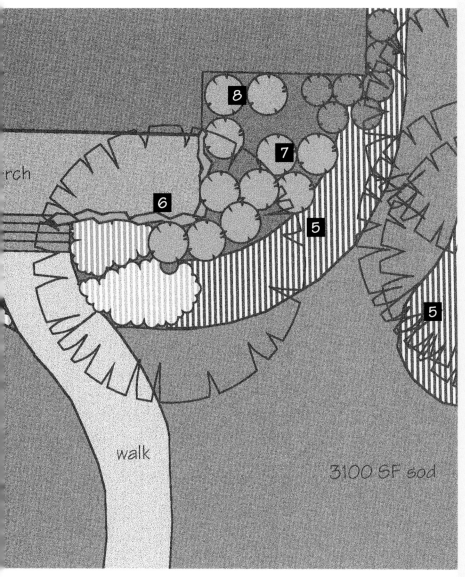

The new design incorporates shrubs, flowers, and ground covers in masses for the greatest impact. Trees add height and color to the landscape, while bold, curving bed lines define and separate the lawn from the plant beds. A good mix of plant textures provides visual interest.

To complete the design, the plan incorporates a selective amount of color. Annuals and perennials line the walkway near the front door and encircle the mailbox, where passersby will appreciate them.

1. Several dwarf yaupon hollies occupy the space under the windows on the left side of the house. These shrubs will never cover the windows, because they grow only 4 feet tall.

2. Nellie R. Stevens holly accents the left corner of the house. This coarse-textured evergreen shrub provides visual weight in the area, while screening the air-conditioning units from view.

3. Dwarf pittosporum surrounds the left side of the porch. This small, medium-textured shrub is well suited to this spot because it grows in a compact, mounded habit.

4. The height and color of crepe myrtle trees help define the left side of the yard.

5. The small, glossy green leaves of Japanese star jasmine provide textural contrast in the lawn. As with most ground covers, Japanese star jasmine is most effective in masses or as a filler in plant beds.

6. Asian sweet autumn clematis, a flowering vine, wraps around the right side of the front porch. Its white, late-summer blooms bring a delicate fragrance to the landscape.

7. The medium-textured foliage and pale summer flowers of dwarf Indian hawthorn highlight the right side of the house. This shrub grows only 4 feet tall.

8. Oakleaf hydrangea, a coarse-textured deciduous shrub with large leaves and showy summer flowers, anchors the planting at the right end of the house.

Plant Profiles

The rich blend of textures and colors around this water feature includes mondo grass, orange coneflower, and dwarf fountain grass, an ornamental grass. A backdrop of evergreens makes the flowers and grass more prominent.

All successful landscape designs use plants for beauty and function. The following pages include 106 popular Southern plants selected by the *Southern Living* garden editors on the basis of the plant's beauty, versatility, and adaptability to various conditions.

Arranged alphabetically by common name, these profiles provide the highlights of each plant to help you choose those needed for your design. The botanical name is also included to avoid confusion.

Plant profiles begin with the **plant type** and suggested **landscape use.** Together, the entries on **features, color,** and **texture** describe the ornamental qualities of the plant. Plant statistics, such as **form, height,** and **width** (or spread), will help you choose plants that fit your site. A summary of the plant's horticultural requirements is given under the entries **light, soil,** and **water.** The information included under **range** will help you choose plants that are adapted to your area. (See the Plant Hardiness Zone Map on page 123.) Finally, other information important to your success is included under **remarks.** However, before purchasing any plants, check with local sources, such as your Extension service or a nursery, to learn about local conditions that may affect a plant or of selections best adapted to your area.

The photos accompanying each profile show you what these plants contribute to the design. Most of the landscape uses listed in the profiles are easily understood. For example, a shade tree provides shade. However, some of the uses require further explanation. The following should help clarify the meaning of these design terms.

Accent. Plants designated as accents usually have a distinctive feature or quality that attracts attention, such as the pearl-like flowers on a Japanese andromeda.

Backdrop (or background). Like a curtain of green, some plants, especially evergreens, can serve as a background for displaying other plants. For example, a bright flower border is attractive against a backdrop of evergreens. Popular background plants include common boxwood and evergreen azaleas.

Border. A border is a large bed of plants containing many different species. Evergreen shrubs usually form the background in a border, with smaller flowering plants filling the remainder of the bed. Popular border plants include beautybush, fountain grass, and foxglove.

Edging. Plants used for edging have a neat, low-growing habit. This allows them to work well around the edge of a bed or a structure, such as a walkway. A popular plant for edging is candytuft.

Foundation planting. A foundation planting is the planting at the base of a home (see page 61). Plants used for this purpose are among the most dependable with many of them being evergreen. Good examples are common boxwood and Japanese aucuba.

Grouping. Sometimes trees and shrubs are especially effective when used in groups. Several dogwoods or redbuds can be planted to create a miniature grove.

Mass planting. Plants are often used in multiples and planted close enough together so that they grow into a solid mass of foliage. This concept, discussed on page 49, is a key component of good design.

Naturalizing. Plants used for naturalizing usually work well in woodland or meadowlike settings. Some tend to multiply and behave as plants in the wild do. A good example is a field of daffodils planted under a large tree. Others, especially native plants such as chokeberry and Piedmont azaleas, are used to recreate a natural setting.

A perfectly clipped low hedge of Japanese boxwood adds to the formality of this garden design.

Screen. A plant screen forms a dense wall of green foliage. Good examples are camellias and Canadian hemlock.

Seasonal color. Plants with a bright show of color in one season provide seasonal color. Annuals such as impatiens and zinnias bring a wide range of color in early and late summer, while a sourwood tree will be a blaze of scarlet in the fall.

Specimen. A specimen plant is usually an individual plant that is representative of its class and is outstanding when used alone. Examples are Chinese elm, chokeberry, and Japanese maple. These plants have an outstanding feature such as showy bark, clusters of red berries, or great fall color.

Requiring little attention, glossy abelia is a reliable border shrub that flowers best in the summer sun.

ABELIA, GLOSSY

❖

Abelia x *grandiflora*

Plant type: semievergreen shrub

Landscape use: hedge, screen, foundation planting

Features: glossy foliage, profuse bell-shaped summer flowers

Color: white blooms, dark green foliage

Height: 3 to 6 feet, depending on selection

Width: 3 to 6 feet

Form: rounded, arching

Texture: fine

Light: full sun

Soil: moist, well drained

Water: medium

Range: Zones 5 to 9

Remarks: tough, drought-tolerant plant; flowers attract butterflies and bees

Ajuga's purple spike flowers appear in mid-April, and its foliage intensifies in color in the fall.

AJUGA

❖

Ajuga reptans

Plant type: evergreen ground cover

Landscape use: ground cover, edging

Features: colorful foliage, early-spring flowers

Color: bluish purple or white blooms; red, bronze, green, or variegated foliage

Height: 3 to 5 inches

Width: 6 to 8 inches

Form: spreading, mat forming

Texture: medium

Light: partial sun to shade

Soil: well drained

Water: low to medium

Range: Zones 2 to 9

Remarks: spreads quickly, may die back in prolonged wet weather, needs excellent drainage

ANDROMEDA, Japanese

❖

Pieris japonica

Plant type: evergreen shrub
Landscape use: accent, naturalizing
Features: exquisite foliage, delicate pearl-like strands of flowers, red new growth
Color: white or pink blooms
Height: 3 to 12 feet
Width: 4 to 6 feet
Form: upright
Texture: fine to medium
Light: partial shade
Soil: rich, moist, well drained, slightly acid
Water: medium
Range: Zones 5 to 8
Remarks: will not tolerate hot, dry conditions

Japanese andromeda is an elegant evergreen shrub prized for its sculptural form and late-winter flowers.

ASPIDISTRA

❖

Aspidistra elatior

Plant type: evergreen ground cover
Landscape use: ground cover, houseplant
Features: oblong, leathery leaves
Height: 2 to 2½ feet
Form: upright
Texture: coarse
Light: shade
Soil: acid, tolerates many different soil conditions
Water: low to medium
Range: Zones 7 to 9
Remarks: does well in deep shade and dry conditions under trees, grows slowly

The upright leaves of aspidistra make it a bold accent in addition to its popularity as a durable ground cover.

AUCUBA, JAPANESE

❖

Aucuba japonica

Plant type: evergreen shrub
Landscape use: screen, foundation planting
Features: large, glossy leaves
Color: green or golden variegated foliage
Height: 3 to 10 feet
Width: 2 to 3 feet
Form: upright
Texture: coarse
Light: partial shade to deep shade
Soil: moist, well drained
Water: medium
Range: Zones 7 to 10
Remarks: a dependable, hardy shrub that has a tropical look

Japanese aucuba is a hardy evergreen that will stay full and handsome in the shade.

AZALEA, FLORIDA FLAME

❖

Azalea austrinum

Plant type: deciduous shrub
Landcape use: accent, naturalizing
Features: fragrant spring flowers
Color: golden yellow to soft orange blooms
Height: 5 to 6 feet
Width: 5 to 6 feet
Form: upright, irregular
Texture: medium
Light: partial shade
Soil: rich, acid, moist, well drained
Water: medium
Range: Zones 7 to 9
Remarks: native to lower South

The flowers of Florida flame azalea bloom in early spring, just before the leaves unfurl.

AZALEA, Kurume Hybrid

Azalea obtusum

Plant type: evergreen shrub
Landscape use: backdrop, hedge, mass or foundation planting
Features: spring flowers
Color: pink, red, orange, or white blooms
Height: 3 to 6 feet
Width: 3 to 6 feet
Form: upright, mounding
Texture: medium
Light: partial shade
Soil: acid, moist, well drained
Water: medium
Range: Zones 7 to 9
Remarks: older plants surprisingly drought tolerant, needs regular watering during first few years

Kurume hybrid azaleas include some of the most vivid azalea colors.

AZALEA, Piedmont

Azalea canescens

Plant type: deciduous shrub
Landscape use: accent
Features: fragrant flowers
Color: white to pink blooms
Height: 10 to 15 feet
Width: 4 to 6 feet
Form: upright, sculptural
Texture: medium
Light: partial sun to shade
Soil: rich, well drained
Water: medium
Range: Zones 5 to 9
Remarks: one of the easiest native azaleas to grow

Piedmont azalea is a widespread native whose fragrance is unmistakable.

Southern Indian hybrid azaleas are the largest of all the evergreen azaleas.

AZALEA, SOUTHERN INDIAN HYBRID

❖

Azalea x *indicum*

Plant type: evergreen shrub
Landscape use: border, mass planting
Features: magnificent spring flowers, graceful form
Color: pink, white, red, purple, or salmon-colored blooms
Height: 6 to 12 feet
Width: 6 to 12 feet
Form: rounded, irregular
Texture: medium
Light: partial shade
Soil: rich, acid, moist, well drained
Water: medium
Range: Zones 7 to 9
Remarks: wide color variety, good privacy hedge

Crimson pygmy barberry is well suited for hot locations and poor soil.

BARBERRY, CRIMSON PYGMY

❖

Berberis thunbergii Crimson Pygmy

Plant type: broadleaf evergreen shrub
Landscape use: foundation planting, low hedge
Features: spiny evergreen foliage, red fruit
Color: red foliage, yellow blooms
Height: 1½ to 2 feet
Width: 3 to 4 feet
Form: rounded, spreading
Texture: fine
Light: full sun
Soil: moist, well drained, slightly acid
Water: medium
Range: Zones 4 to 8
Remarks: tolerates urban conditions well, color is best in full sun

BEAUTYBUSH
❖

Kolkwitzia amabilis

Plant type: deciduous shrub
Landscape use: accent, border, specimen
Features: graceful form, trumpet-shaped
late-spring flowers
Color: pink blooms
Height: 8 to 15 feet
Width: 6 to 10 feet
Form: upright, arching with cascading
branches
Texture: medium
Light: full sun to partial shade
Soil: well drained
Water: low
Range: Zones 4 to 8
Remarks: grows quickly, tolerates acid or
alkaline soil, prune oldest limbs at the
base to maintain fullness

Beautybush needs plenty of room to spread its branches, which are loaded with blossoms in spring.

BEECH, AMERICAN
❖

Fagus grandifolia

Plant type: deciduous tree
Landscape use: accent, shade tree
Features: beautiful form, foliage, and bark
Color: golden bronze foliage
Height: 50 to 70 feet
Spread: 40 to 60 feet
Form: rounded
Texture: coarse
Light: full sun to partial shade
Soil: moist, well drained
Water: medium
Range: Zones 3 to 9
Remarks: native, slow-growing tree; casts
deep shade; do not disturb roots by tilling

American beech is a large native tree noted for the parchmentlike leaves it retains all winter.

BEGONIA, Hardy

❖

Begonia grandis

Plant type: perennial
Landscape use: summer color, foliage
Features: colorful, heart-shaped leaves;
    late-summer flowers
Color: pink blooms
Height: 1 to 2 feet
Width: 1 to 2 feet
Light: partial shade
Soil: rich, light, well drained
Water: medium
Range: Zones 6 to 8
Remarks: nice texture for shady areas,
    even when not in bloom

*Hardy begonia, a faithful perennial with
old-fashioned charm, blooms in the shade.*

BIRCH, River

❖

Betula nigra

Plant type: deciduous tree
Landscape use: accent, foundation planting
Features: shaggy, multicolored bark
Color: various shades of beige bark
Height: 40 to 60 feet
Spread: 40 to 60 feet
Form: upright
Texture: medium
Light: full sun
Soil: moist to wet, acid
Water: medium to high
Range: Zones 4 to 9
Remarks: fast-growing native tree, toler-
    ates poorly drained soil, withstands dry
    conditions

*River birch often has multiple trunks, which
show off its light-colored, shaggy bark.*

BLUE FESCUE

❖

Festuca glauca

Plant type: ornamental grass
Landscape use: ground cover, accent
Features: fine-textured, silver-blue foliage
Form: upright, clumping
Texture: fine
Height: 4 to 18 inches
Light: full sun to partial shade
Soil: well drained
Water: low
Range: Zones 4 to 7
Remarks: drought resistant; doesn't like hot, humid weather; shabby foliage must be cut back in fall

Aptly named, blue fescue makes an eye-catching ground cover.

BOXWOOD, COMMON

❖

Buxus sempervirens

Plant type: evergreen shrub
Landscape use: hedge, screen, foundation planting
Features: stately form and foliage
Color: dark green foliage
Height: 3 to 15 feet
Width: 3 to 15 feet
Form: rounded
Texture: fine
Light: partial sun
Soil: rich, well drained
Water: medium
Range: Zones 5 to 8
Remarks: long-lived shrub, dense foliage, indispensable formal planting

Common boxwood is one of the classic choices for hedges in formal and traditional landscapes.

CALADIUM

❖

Caladium x *hortulanum*

Plant type: annual bulb
Landscape use: seasonal color
Features: large patterned leaves from spring until frost
Color: green foliage with white, red, or pink patterns
Height: 10 to 24 inches
Width: 10 to 24 inches
Light: full sun to shade
Soil: moist
Water: medium
Range: Zones 4 to 10
Remarks: types that grow in full sun need extra water

Caladiums are a popular annual for shade; some selections also tolerate sun.

CAMELLIA, COMMON

❖

Camellia japonica

Plant type: evergreen shrub
Landscape use: accent, screen, foundation planting
Features: glossy evergreen foliage, porcelain-like flowers
Color: white, pink, red, or bicolored blooms
Height: 10 to 15 feet
Width: 6 to 10 feet
Form: upright, pyramidal
Texture: coarse
Light: partial shade
Soil: moist, well drained, slightly acid
Water: medium
Range: Zones 7 to 9
Remarks: provides brilliant color in winter and early spring, will not tolerate alkaline soil

Common camellia grows to nearly the size of a small tree.

CAMELLIA, Sasanqua

Camellia sasanqua

Plant type: evergreen shrub

Landscape use: accent, espalier, hedge, screen

Features: glossy evergreen foliage, profuse flowers

Color: white, pink, or red blooms

Height: 6 to 10 feet, sometimes 15 feet

Width: 4 to 8 feet

Form: rounded, irregular

Texture: medium

Light: partial shade

Soil: moist, well drained, slightly acid

Water: medium

Range: Zones 7 to 9

Remarks: popular evergreen shrub valued for its fall blooms

Sasanqua camellia is one of the few shrubs that blooms in the fall.

CANDYTUFT, Evergreen

Iberis sempervirens

Plant type: perennial

Landscape use: border, edging, ground cover

Features: clusters of early-spring flowers atop evergreen foliage

Color: white blooms

Height: 4 to 12 inches

Width: 6 to 8 inches

Light: full sun to partial shade

Soil: well drained

Water: low

Range: Zones 3 to 9

Remarks: if sheared after flowering, will often rebloom in fall in areas with a long growing season

Candytuft, a creeping evergreen perennial, covers itself with white blooms in early spring.

CHERRY, YOSHINO

❖

Prunus yedoensis

Plant type: deciduous tree
Landscape use: accent, small shade tree
Features: spring flowers; smooth, shiny bark
Color: white to pink blooms
Height: 15 to 25 feet
Spread: 15 to 20 feet
Form: upright, spreading
Texture: medium
Light: full sun to partial shade
Soil: well drained
Water: low to medium
Range: Zones 5 to 8
Remarks: short-lived tree that survives only 15 to 20 years

Yoshino cherry fills the garden with pastel blossoms in the spring.

CHOKEBERRY

❖

Aronia arbutifolia

Plant type: deciduous shrub
Landscape use: accent, mass planting, naturalizing
Features: brilliant fall color, clusters of red berries
Color: red berries
Height: 6 to 10 feet
Width: 6 to 8 feet
Form: upright, vase shaped
Texture: medium
Light: full sun to partial shade
Soil: wet to dry, fertile to poor
Water: low to high
Range: Zones 6 to 9
Remarks: native shrub, berries last through winter because birds ignore them

The showy red berries of chokeberry appear in late summer but are most striking when the plant's leaves drop in the fall.

CLEMATIS,
ASIAN SWEET AUTUMN
❖
Clematis paniculata

Plant type: semievergreen vine
Landscape use: fence, mailbox, or trellis plant
Features: delicate, fragrant late-summer flowers
Color: white blooms
Height: climbs 10 to 30 feet
Form: climbing
Texture: medium
Light: full sun
Soil: well drained, tolerates many soil types
Water: low to medium
Range: Zones 5 to 9
Remarks: lightweight, easy to grow, climbs by winding, can be invasive

Asian sweet autumn clematis, a fast-growing vine with showy white flowers, also grows wild throughout the South.

CLEYERA, JAPANESE
❖
Ternstroemia gymnanthera

Plant type: evergreen shrub
Landscape use: accent, screen, foundation planting
Features: glossy foliage, tidy growth habit
Color: bronze new growth
Height: 8 to 10 feet
Width: 5 to 6 feet
Form: upright, rounded
Texture: medium
Light: full sun to partial shade
Soil: well drained
Water: medium
Range: Zones 7 to 9
Remarks: severe cold can cause leaf drop, needs excellent drainage

Japanese cleyera is characterized by glossy, deep green leaves that take on a red to purple tint in cold weather.

COLEUS

Coleus species

Plant type: annual
Landscape use: seasonal color
Features: multicolored foliage
Color: white, yellow, red to pink, copper, dark green to chartreuse, variegated
Height: 6 to 36 inches
Width: 1 to 3 feet
Light: full sun to shade
Soil: moist, fertile to poor
Water: medium to high
Range: Zones 3 to 10
Remarks: keep plant compact by pinching off blooms as they appear

The intense red foliage of coleus adds constant color to the garden from spring until frost.

CONEFLOWER, Orange

Rudbeckia fulgida

Plant type: perennial
Landscape use: seasonal color, flower border
Features: profuse, colorful daisylike flowers
Color: golden yellow
Height: 2 to 3 feet
Width: 12 to 16 inches
Light: full sun to light shade
Soil: well drained
Water: medium
Range: Zones 3 to 10
Remarks: blooms from midsummer until frost, suitable for both wildflower gardens and cultivated borders, Goldsturm is most common selection

A long-lived perennial, orange coneflower will bloom without fail year after year.

CONEFLOWER, Purple

❖

Echinacea purpurea

Plant type: perennial
Landscape use: seasonal color, flower border, naturalizing
Features: tall stalks, beautiful summer flowers, prominent cone
Color: lavender or pink blooms, brown to orange cone
Height: 2 to 4 feet
Width: 2 to 3 feet
Light: full sun to partial shade
Soil: well drained
Water: medium
Range: Zones 3 to 10
Remarks: good cut flower, attracts butterflies, will reseed

Purple coneflower, a dependable native, is one of the easiest perennials to grow.

COREOPSIS

❖

Coreopsis species

Plant type: perennial
Landscape use: seasonal color, flower border
Features: daisylike flowers
Color: pale to golden yellow blooms
Height: 10 to 36 inches
Width: 1 to 2 feet
Light: full sun
Soil: poor, well drained
Water: low
Range: Zones 4 to 9
Remarks: several species available, blooms most abundantly in spring, remove spent flowers to prolong blooming into summer and fall

Coreopsis offers a show of color all summer yet requires only minimum care.

The branches of low, spreading selections of cotoneaster will cascade over a wall or root where they touch ground if used as a ground cover.

COTONEASTER

❖

Cotoneaster species

Plant type: evergreen or deciduous shrub
Landscape use: ground cover, low shrub, accent, espalier
Features: small spring flowers followed by abundant fruit
Color: white, pink, or red blooms; red berries
Height: 1 to 10 feet
Width: 3 to 6 feet
Form: irregular, arching, spreading
Texture: fine
Light: full sun to partial shade
Soil: moist, well drained
Water: medium
Range: Zones 4 to 8
Remarks: many species and selections available, shop carefully for types recommended for your area

With its soft, crepelike blooms and handsome bark, crepe myrtle is one of the South's most widely planted small trees.

CREPE MYRTLE

❖

Lagerstroemia indica and hybrids

Plant type: deciduous tree
Landscape use: accent, small shade tree
Features: beautiful summer flowers, showy bark
Color: white, pink, red, or lavender blooms
Height: 3 to 25 feet
Spread: 15 to 25 feet
Form: upright, multitrunked
Texture: medium
Light: full sun
Soil: well drained
Water: low
Range: Zones 7 to 9
Remarks: long-lived, durable, excellent for small spaces, plant new hybrids for disease resistance

DAFFODIL

❖

Narcissus species

Plant type: perennial (bulb)

Landscape use: accent, flower border, naturalizing

Features: bright, nodding, early-spring flowers

Color: yellow or white blooms

Height: 4 to 18 inches

Width: 3 to 12 inches

Light: full sun to partial shade

Soil: well drained

Water: let soil dry between thorough waterings

Range: Zones 4 to 9

Remarks: fertilize in fall and again after flowers bloom; let leaves die down on their own, do not cut or tie them

Daffodils are the most dependable of the spring-flowering bulbs, lasting for many years with little attention.

DAYLILY

❖

Hemerocallis species and hybrids

Plant type: perennial

Landscape use: ground cover, flower border, naturalizing

Features: showy summer flowers, grassy foliage

Color: yellow, orange, pink, mauve, red, or purple blooms

Height: 1 to 4 feet

Width: 1 to 3 feet

Light: full sun to partial shade

Soil: well drained

Water: medium

Range: Zones 3 to 10

Remarks: some landscape-type daylilies bloom again in late summer and fall

Daylilies bloom for several years before they must be divided.

Dogwood, a flowering native tree, does best in partial shade and moist but well-drained soil.

DOGWOOD, FLOWERING
❖
Cornus florida

Plant type: deciduous tree
Landscape use: specimen, grouping
Features: spring flowers, excellent red fall color
Color: white or pink blooms, red berries
Height: 10 to 20 feet
Spread: 15 to 20 feet
Form: upright with prominent horizontal branches
Texture: medium
Light: partial shade
Soil: rich, slightly acid, moist, well drained
Water: medium
Range: Zones 5 to 9
Remarks: native, works well in shade of pines and other large trees

DOGWOOD, KOUSA
❖
Cornus kousa

Plant type: deciduous tree
Landscape use: accent
Features: late-spring flowers, red to purple autumn color, attractive winter bark
Color: white blooms
Height: 20 to 30 feet
Spread: 20 to 30 feet
Form: upright, oval
Texture: medium
Light: partial shade
Soil: rich, moist, well drained
Water: medium
Range: Zones 5 to 8
Remarks: bright red late-summer fruit

Blooming later than flowering dogwood, Kousa dogwood displays its white blooms in May or early June.

ELM, CHINESE

Ulmus parvifolia

Plant type: deciduous tree
Landscape use: specimen, shade tree
Features: graceful branches, beautiful mottled bark
Color: gray, green, orange, or brown bark
Height: 40 to 50 feet, sometimes 70 feet
Spread: 30 to 40 feet
Form: rounded, open
Texture: fine to medium
Light: full sun
Soil: well drained
Water: low
Range: Zones 4 to 9
Remarks: grows quickly, tolerates urban conditions

A popular tree for rural or city landscapes, Chinese elm tolerates poor soil and is resistant to Dutch elm disease.

EUONYMUS, WINGED

Euonymus alata

Plant type: deciduous shrub
Landscape use: informal hedge, mass planting, backdrop for flower border
Features: green in summer, eye-catching brilliance in fall
Color: red fall foliage
Height: 6 to 20 feet
Width: 10 to 15 feet
Form: vase shaped
Texture: fine
Light: full sun
Soil: well drained
Water: low
Range: Zones 3 to 8
Remarks: needs growing room, dwarf winged euonymus is most common selection

Dwarf winged euonymus is commonly called burning bush because of its brilliant red fall color.

FATSHEDERA

❖

Fatshedera x *lizei*

Plant type: evergreen vinelike shrub
Landscape use: wall, fence, or trellis plant
Features: dark green leathery leaves with deep lobes
Height: climbs 8 to 10 feet
Form: spreading
Texture: coarse
Light: partial sun to shade
Soil: well drained
Water: low to medium
Range: Zones 8 to 10
Remarks: needs staking or other support, cannot tolerate poor drainage

Although fatshedera's heavy vines must be supported, its impressive, large leaves make it worth the effort.

FIG, CREEPING

❖

Ficus pumila

Plant type: evergreen vine
Landscape use: wall or fence plant
Features: small, rough leaves with close, dense growth pattern
Height: climbs to 60 feet
Form: climbing
Texture: fine
Light: full sun to partial shade
Soil: well drained
Water: low to medium
Range: Zones 8 to 10
Remarks: vigorous, can be rampant, variegated selection available

Creeping fig clings to most surfaces, creating a fine-textured mat of green foliage year-round.

FORSYTHIA

❖

Forsythia x *intermedia*

Plant type: deciduous shrub
Landscape use: informal hedge, specimen
Features: arching sprays of flowers; thick, dark green foliage
Color: yellow blooms
Height: 3 to 10 feet
Width: 5 to 12 feet
Form: arching, spreading
Texture: medium
Light: full sun
Soil: well drained
Water: medium
Range: Zones 5 to 9
Remarks: blooms in early spring, needs growing room, best in natural form

The bright yellow flowers of forsythia appear in late winter, signaling the arrival of spring.

FOUNTAIN GRASS

❖

Pennisetum species

Plant type: perennial ornamental grass
Landscape use: accent, ground cover, border
Features: bronze fall plumes, fountainlike foliage
Color: green or red leaves
Height: 1 to 4 feet
Width: 1 to 3 feet
Form: upright, fountainlike
Texture: fine
Light: full sun to partial shade
Soil: well drained
Water: low
Range: Zones 4 to 9
Remarks: blooms best in full sun, cut back browned leaves in late winter, red-leafed *Pennisetum setaceum* is an annual

Fountain grass offers a wispy softness wherever it is used.

FOXGLOVE

❖

Digitalis purpurea

Plant type: biennial
Landscape use: seasonal color in backgrounds, borders
Features: spires of bell-like flowers
Color: white, pink, or purple blooms
Height: 2 to 7 feet
Width: 2 feet
Light: morning sun or partial shade
Soil: fertile, well drained
Water: medium
Range: Zones 4 to 10
Remarks: large fall-planted transplants will bloom the next spring (small ones, too, if soil is rich), plants may reseed but seldom live more than one year

Although short-lived, the dramatic spikes of foxglove are worth the time it takes to replant each year.

GERANIUM

❖

Pelargonium x hortortum

Plant type: annual
Landscape use: seasonal color for pots, planters, and borders
Features: large clusters of flowers from early summer to frost
Color: white, pink, scarlet, salmon, orange, or lavender blooms
Height: 1 to 2 feet
Width: 1 to 2 feet
Light: full sun, afternoon shade in summer
Soil: well drained, fertile
Water: medium to high
Range: Zones 3 to 10
Remarks: blooms may slow in summer heat; continue to water and fertilize through summer for good fall show

Geraniums are as much at home in containers as they are in a flowerbed.

GINKGO

❖

Ginkgo biloba

Plant type: deciduous tree
Landscape use: specimen, shade tree
Features: stiff, angular growth; exquisite fall color
Color: golden yellow foliage in autumn
Height: 50 to 80 feet
Spread: 30 to 40 feet
Form: rounded to spreading
Texture: medium
Light: full sun
Soil: well drained, tolerates alkaline soil
Water: medium to low
Range: Zones 3 to 9
Remarks: disease free, slow growing, female trees produce fruit with strong odor

Ginkgo is a stately, rugged tree prized for its brilliant yellow fall color.

GLADIOLUS, HARDY

❖

Gladiolus byzantinus

Plant type: perennial
Landscape use: seasonal color for beds and borders
Features: spikes of spring flowers
Color: magenta blooms
Height: 2 to 2½ feet
Width: 1 to 2 feet
Light: full sun
Soil: well drained
Water: low to medium
Range: Zones 6 to 9
Remarks: best used in clusters, blooms from bottom to top, may be hard to find but can substitute florist and dwarf gladiolus

An old-fashioned Southern favorite, hardy gladiolus is a more dependable perennial than florist gladiolus but difficult to find.

GOLDENRAIN TREE

❖

Koelreuteria paniculata

Plant type: deciduous tree
Landscape use: accent, small shade tree
Features: sprays of summer flowers,
    parchment-colored seedpods
Color: bright yellow blooms
Height: 15 to 40 feet
Spread: 15 to 30 feet
Form: upright, spreading
Texture: fine
Light: full sun
Soil: well drained
Water: medium to low
Range: Zones 5 to 9
Remarks: great patio tree; heat tolerant;
    tolerates poor, sandy, and alkaline soil

Goldenrain tree may be the only tree to sport yellow blossoms in summer.

HELENIUM

❖

Helenium species

Plant type: perennial
Landscape use: seasonal color for borders
Features: daisylike late-summer flowers
Color: red, orange, or yellow blooms
Height: 3 to 5 feet
Width: 2 feet
Light: full sun
Soil: any type, well drained
Water: low
Range: Zones 3 to 9
Remarks: do not fertilize, divide clumps
    every two to three years

A tall, colorful perennial in the fall garden, helenium does well in sunny spots with poor soil.

HELIOPSIS

❖

Heliopsis species

Plant type: perennial
Landscape use: seasonal color, borders
Features: daisylike flowers from June to September
Color: orange-yellow blooms
Height: 2 to 5 feet
Width: 2 to 4 feet
Light: full sun
Soil: well drained
Water: low
Range: Zones 3 to 9
Remarks: several selections available, good as cut flowers

Heliopsis is a native, hardy perennial that brings bright orange-yellow flowers to sunny beds in summer and fall.

HEMLOCK, CANADIAN

❖

Tsuga canadensis

Plant type: evergreen tree
Landscape use: screen, specimen
Features: fine, needlelike foliage; graceful form
Height: 40 to 70 feet
Spread: 25 to 35 feet
Form: pyramidal
Texture: fine
Light: shade in South, full sun in North
Soil: fertile, well drained
Water: medium
Range: Zones 3 to 7
Remarks: good screen, native, keep young trees moist during drought

A perfect garden backdrop, Canadian hemlock's needles are lime green when they emerge, changing quickly to dark, glossy green.

HICKORY, SHAGBARK

❖

Carya ovata

Plant type: deciduous tree
Landscape use: shade tree
Features: golden fall color, deep green foliage
Height: 60 to 80 feet
Spread: 30 to 40 feet
Form: oval
Texture: coarse
Light: full sun
Soil: well drained
Water: low to medium
Range: Zones 4 to 9
Remarks: native, use where hickory nuts can fall into mulch or are not a maintenance problem

Although hard to find in nurseries, shagbark hickory's fall color makes it a good choice for a large, open property.

HOLLY, BURFORD

❖

Ilex cornuta Burfordii

Plant type: evergreen shrub
Landscape use: accent, screen, mass planting
Features: glossy evergreen foliage, large red berries in fall and winter
Height: 15 to 20 feet
Width: 10 to 15 feet
Form: rounded
Texture: coarse
Light: full sun
Soil: well drained
Water: low
Range: Zones 7 to 9
Remarks: drought tolerant, grows quickly, great for screening, too large for foundation plantings

Transform an older Burford holly into a small tree by pruning its lower limbs.

HOLLY, DWARF YAUPON

❖

Ilex vomitoria Nana

Plant type: evergreen shrub
Landscape use: foundation planting, low hedge, ground cover
Features: small, shiny leaves; low, cushionlike growth habit
Height: 3 to 4 feet
Width: 3 to 4 feet
Form: rounded, spreading
Texture: fine
Light: full sun to light shade
Soil: tolerates sand, clay, and alkaline soil
Water: low
Range: Zones 7 to 10
Remarks: withstands heat and drought

One of the best and most reliable small evergreen shrubs, dwarf yaupon holly is a good alternative to boxwood, especially in the warmer regions.

HOLLY, FOSTER

❖

Ilex x *attenuata* Foster #2

Plant type: evergreen tree
Landscape use: accent, screen, specimen
Features: narrow, dark green leaves; profuse red berries in fall and winter
Height: 25 to 40 feet
Spread: 10 to 15 feet
Form: rigid, pyramidal
Texture: medium
Light: full sun to partial shade
Soil: moist, well drained, acid
Water: medium
Range: Zones 6 to 9
Remarks: hardy evergreen, good for screening

When planted close together, Foster hollies will grow into a dense evergreen mass of foliage and winter berries.

HOLLY, Heller Japanese

❖

Ilex crenata Helleri

Plant type: evergreen shrub

Landscape use: foundation or mass planting, ground cover, container plant

Features: dense, deep green foliage; low, nearly flat-topped shape

Height: 2 to 3 feet

Width: 3 to 4 feet

Form: spreading

Texture: fine

Light: full sun to partial shade

Soil: fertile, moist, well drained

Water: medium

Range: Zones 5 to 7

Remarks: finicky about moisture, will not tolerate poorly drained locations or extreme drought

Heller Japanese holly is a slow-growing small shrub that works well as a background for colorful low-growing flowers.

HOLLY, Nellie R. Stevens

❖

Ilex x Nellie R. Stevens

Plant type: evergreen shrub

Landscape use: screen

Features: dark black-green, glossy foliage

Color: red berries in fall and winter

Height: 10 to 20 feet

Width: 6 to 12 feet

Form: upright

Texture: coarse

Light: full sun

Soil: well drained

Water: low to medium

Range: Zones 7 to 9

Remarks: needs a Chinese holly nearby in order to pollinate and produce berries

Nellie R. Stevens holly is a large evergreen shrub that has the darkest green foliage of all the hollies.

HOLLY, ROTUNDA

❖

Ilex cornuta Rotunda

Plant type: evergreen shrub
Landscape use: ground cover, mass or foundation planting
Features: 5- to 7-spined glossy green leaves
Height: 3 to 4 feet
Width: 6 to 8 feet
Form: low, rounded
Texture: coarse
Light: full sun to light shade
Soil: well drained
Water: low
Range: Zones 7 to 9
Remarks: very dense and prickly; almost indestructible; good for hot, sunny areas with poor soil

The glossy leaves and rigid, compact form of Rotunda holly give this rugged shrub a flawless appearance.

HOSTA

❖

Hosta species

Plant type: perennial
Landscape use: borders, ground cover, seasonal color
Features: lush, bold-textured foliage from spring to fall
Color: chartreuse, blue-green, medium green, or variegated leaves
Height: 3 to 48 inches
Width: 3 to 48 inches
Light: partial shade to full shade
Soil: rich, well drained
Water: medium
Range: Zones 3 to 8
Remarks: mass as ground cover, use with ferns in shady areas for textural accent

Hosta is a long-lived, shade-loving perennial.

HYDRANGEA, Oakleaf

❖

Hydrangea quercifolia

Plant type: deciduous shrub

Landscape use: mass planting, naturalizing

Features: large flowers, red fall color, peeling bark

Color: white blooms

Height: 4 to 10 feet

Width: 10 feet

Form: irregular, mounding

Texture: coarse

Light: full sun to partial shade

Soil: moist, well drained, acid

Water: low

Range: Zones 5 to 9

Remarks: good drainage essential, native to shady woodlands of Southeast

Oakleaf hydrangea is valued for its large foliage and striking oversized flowers that bloom in summer.

IMPATIENS

❖

Impatiens wallerana

Plant type: annual

Landscape use: seasonal color for beds, borders, and containers

Features: nonstop flowers from spring until frost

Color: white, pink, lavender, orange, red, or purple blooms

Height: 6 to 24 inches

Width: 6 to 24 inches

Light: morning sun, partial shade to full shade

Soil: moist, well drained

Water: high

Range: Zones 5 to 9

Remarks: wilts in hot afternoon sun, keep soil evenly moist, double-flowered types available

Available in an abundance of colors, impatiens bloom profusely, creating dazzling mounds of flowers.

INDIAN HAWTHORN

❖

Raphiolepis indica

Plant type: evergreen shrub
Landscape use: accent, ground cover, mass or foundation planting
Features: profuse, fragrant flowers in spring; dark green foliage
Color: white or pink blooms
Height: 4 to 10 feet
Width: 4 to 10 feet
Form: rounded, spreading
Texture: medium
Light: full sun
Soil: tolerates alkaline soil, needs good drainage
Water: low to medium
Range: Zones 8 to 10
Remarks: tolerates poor, sandy soil and salt spray

Indian hawthorn is a tough but pretty shrub that endures the heat and poor soils of the coastal South.

IVY, ALGERIAN

❖

Hedera canariensis

Plant type: evergreen vine
Landscape use: ground cover, vine
Features: dark green leaves, black berries in fall
Height: 1 foot as ground cover, 90 feet as vine
Form: vining
Texture: coarse
Light: full sun to partial shade
Soil: rich
Water: low to medium
Range: Zones 8 to 10
Remarks: grows quickly, variegated form works well in summer mixed planters in all zones

Algerian ivy, which has larger leaves than its cousin English ivy, is best suited for the lower South.

IVY, BOSTON

Parthenocissus tricuspidata

Plant type: deciduous vine
Landscape use: accent, climbing plant
Features: brilliant red fall color
Height: climbs to 60 feet
Form: vining
Texture: medium
Light: sun to partial shade
Soil: rich, well drained
Water: medium
Range: Zones 4 to 8
Remarks: grows fast, black berries in summer attract birds, clings to surfaces

Boston ivy will climb to the top of a wall by sending out many runners.

IVY, ENGLISH

Hedera helix

Plant type: evergreen vine
Landscape use: ground cover, climbing plant for walls and fences
Features: classic ivy-shaped foliage
Height: 6 to 12 inches as a ground cover
Form: vining
Texture: medium
Light: partial shade to shade
Soil: well drained
Water: medium
Range: Zones 4 to 9
Remarks: tolerates acid or alkaline soil; vigorous, but grows slowly at first; makes a dense cover; trim old leaves as needed; can climb to 90 feet; clings to surfaces

English ivy is a medium-textured vine that contrasts nicely with grass or other finer-textured ground covers.

JASMINE, Confederate

❖

Trachelospermum jasminoides

Plant type: evergreen vine
Landscape use: ground cover; trellis, arbor, or mailbox plant
Features: fragrant white flowers, leathery dark blue-green leaves
Height: climbs 10 to 20 feet
Form: vining
Texture: medium
Light: partial shade
Soil: moist, fertile, well drained
Water: low to medium
Range: Zones 8 to 10
Remarks: fast growing, makes an open ground cover, not as dense as Japanese star jasmine

Confederate jasmine, with its sweet-smelling white blooms, can add drama to your trellis, arbor, or mailbox in late spring.

JASMINE, Japanese Star

❖

Trachelospermum asiaticum

Plant type: evergreen vine
Landscape use: ground cover, vine
Features: glossy, dark green foliage
Height: climbs to 12 feet
Form: vining, mat forming
Texture: fine
Light: full sun to deep shade
Soil: well drained
Water: low
Range: Zones 7 to 10
Remarks: will fill in faster as ground cover if mulched with 2 to 3 inches of compost

Although it is a vine, Japanese star jasmine makes an excellent ground cover if sheared.

JUNIPER, ANDORRA CREEPING

❖

Juniperus horizontalis Plumosa

Plant type: evergreen shrub and ground cover
Landscape use: ground cover, mass or seaside planting
Features: stiff, upright branches that turn maroon in winter
Color: green to burgundy in winter
Height: 2 feet
Width: 3 to 4 feet
Form: spreading
Texture: fine
Light: full sun
Soil: poor to fertile, well drained
Water: low
Range: Zones 3 to 8
Remarks: requires excellent drainage

Although green in summer, andorra creeping juniper takes on a burgundy hue in winter.

JUNIPER, SHORE

❖

Juniperus conferta

Plant type: evergreen shrub and ground cover
Landscape use: ground cover; mass, hillside, or seaside planting
Features: needlelike leaves, creeping and cascading stems
Height: 1½ to 2 feet
Width: 3 to 9 feet
Form: spreading
Texture: fine
Light: full sun
Soil: poor to fertile, well drained
Water: low
Range: Zones 6 to 10
Remarks: tolerates drought, sandy soil, and salt spray

An attractive, fine-textured shrub or ground cover, shore juniper does best in full sun and well-drained soil.

KERRIA, Japanese

❖

Kerria japonica

Plant type: deciduous shrub
Landscape use: border, mass planting
Features: spring flowers, green stems in winter
Color: golden yellow blooms
Height: 5 to 8 feet
Width: 5 to 12 feet
Form: upright, arching
Texture: medium
Light: partial sun
Soil: moist, fertile, well drained
Water: medium
Range: Zones 4 to 8
Remarks: loose, open form; needs room to drape

Japanese kerria, a sprawling, old-fashioned shrub, lights up with golden blooms in early spring.

LENTEN ROSE

❖

Helleborus orientalis

Plant type: perennial
Landscape use: ground cover, seasonal color, naturalizing
Features: nodding, skirtlike flowers; rosettelike evergreen foliage
Color: cream, pink, or burgundy blooms
Height: 1 to 1½ feet
Width: 1 to 1½ feet
Light: shade
Soil: neutral, well drained
Water: medium
Range: Zones 4 to 8
Remarks: blooms from winter to early spring, will reseed to form colonies

Left alone, Lenten rose will reseed to create a stunning naturalistic cover.

LEYLAND CYPRESS

❖

x *Cupressocyparis leylandii*

Plant type: evergreen tree
Landscape use: screen
Features: dense, dark green foliage
Height: 50 to 60 feet, sometimes 100 feet
Spread: 10 to 15 feet
Form: narrow, columnar
Texture: fine
Light: full sun
Soil: well drained
Water: low to medium
Range: Zones 6 to 10
Remarks: grows quickly, thrives in many
    soil conditions, excellent evergreen screen

These young Leyland cypress will quickly grow into a dense screen.

LIGUSTRUM

❖

Ligustrum japonicum

Plant type: evergreen shrub
Landscape use: accent, mass or screen
    planting, tree-form shrub
Features: glossy evergreen foliage, white
    flower spikes, profuse blue berries
Height: 6 to 18 feet
Width: 6 to 8 feet
Form: upright, sculptural
Texture: fine
Light: full sun
Soil: well drained
Water: medium
Range: Zones 7 to 10
Remarks: fast-growing, long-lived shrub;
    thrives in high heat and dry soil

Ligustrum is often used like a small tree for tight places in the landscape.

LILY-OF-THE-VALLEY

❖

Convallaria majalis

Plant type: perennial
Landscape use: seasonal blooms for beds and borders, seasonal ground cover
Features: fragrant, bell-shaped flowers; large leaves
Color: white blooms
Height: 6 to 15 inches
Width: 6 to 12 inches
Light: partial shade to shade
Soil: fertile, well drained
Water: medium
Range: Zones 2 to 7
Remarks: ideal woodland or border plant, spreads slowly, plant collector's treasure

Multiplying by underground stems, lily-of-the-valley will spread farther each spring.

LIRIOPE

❖

Liriope muscari

Plant type: evergreen ground cover
Landscape use: ground cover, good container plant
Features: grasslike foliage, spikes of purple-blue flowers in late summer
Height: 8 to 18 inches
Form: spreading
Texture: fine to medium
Light: full sun to shade
Soil: tolerates wet, dry, acid, and alkaline soil
Water: low
Range: Zones 4 to 9
Remarks: green and variegated foliage available

Liriope grows into a dense cover that requires little maintenance. Just shear the old leaves in late winter.

LOQUAT

❖

Eriobotrya japonica

Plant type: evergreen tree
Landscape use: accent, specimen, fruit tree
Features: large, coarse foliage; small, fragrant, white flowers; small, oval fruit in spring
Color: white blooms, orange fruit
Height: 15 to 25 feet
Spread: 12 to 20 feet
Form: rounded
Texture: coarse
Light: full sun
Soil: well drained
Water: low to medium
Range: Zones 8 to 10
Remarks: produces delicious fruit in Zones 9 and 10, creates dense shade

Loquat is an attractive, small tree whose large leaves are reminiscent of Southern magnolia.

MAGNOLIA, SOUTHERN

❖

Magnolia grandiflora

Plant type: evergreen tree
Landscape use: specimen, screen
Features: large, glossy leaves; 6- to 10-inch wide fragrant summer flowers
Color: white blooms
Height: 20 to 80 feet
Spread: 12 to 50 feet
Form: upright, pyramidal
Texture: coarse
Light: full sun to partial shade
Soil: well drained
Water: low
Range: Zones 6 to 10
Remarks: native, tolerates sandy soil and salt spray, leaf drop in spring is normal

Let Southern magnolia's lower limbs grow close to the ground; it is almost impossible to grow anything under it.

MAHONIA, LEATHERLEAF
❖
Mahonia bealei

Plant type: evergreen shrub
Landscape use: accent, foundation planting
Features: hollylike leaves; fragrant, late-winter flowers
Color: yellow blooms, purple-blue fruit
Height: 6 to 10 feet
Width: 6 to 8 feet
Form: upright, sculptural
Texture: coarse
Light: partial shade to full shade
Soil: moist, well drained
Water: low to medium
Range: Zones 6 to 9
Remarks: to maintain fullness, cut tallest one or two canes to the ground each year

Leatherleaf mahonia takes on a sculptural form even as a young plant.

MAPLE, JAPANESE
❖
Acer palmatum

Plant type: deciduous tree
Landscape use: accent, specimen, container or small patio tree
Features: exquisite foliage, small stature
Color: dependable red or gold fall foliage
Height: 3 to 30 feet
Spread: 2 to 20 feet
Form: upright with strong horizontal branches
Texture: fine to medium
Light: full sun to partial shade
Soil: moist, well drained, acid
Water: medium
Range: Zones 5 to 8
Remarks: selections vary in size, form, leaf color, and texture

Japanese maple is a small, long-lived tree that always has brilliant fall color.

MAPLE, RED

❖

Acer rubrum

Plant type: deciduous tree
Landscape use: shade tree
Features: spreading canopy, brilliant fall color
Color: red blooms, red fall foliage
Height: 40 to 60 feet
Spread: 40 to 60 feet
Form: upright, rounded
Texture: medium
Light: full sun
Soil: any type, tolerates wet soil
Water: medium to high
Range: Zones 3 to 9
Remarks: native; grows quickly; Autumn Flame, Red Sunset, and October Glory have best fall color

Red maple provides summer shade and glorious fall color.

MAPLE, SUGAR

❖

Acer saccharum

Plant type: deciduous tree
Landscape use: shade tree
Features: superb form, adaptability, radiant fall color
Color: gold to orange fall foliage
Height: 60 to 80 feet
Spread: 40 to 50 feet
Form: upright, rounded
Texture: medium
Light: full sun
Soil: rich, loose, well drained
Water: medium
Range: Zones 4 to 7
Remarks: grows slowly, long-lived, plants will not grow beneath it, avoid planting near paving

Sugar maple, a popular native shade tree, needs room to spread.

MELAMPODIUM

❖

Melampodium paludosum

Plant type: annual
Landscape use: seasonal color
Features: mounding growth habit, bright green leaves, star-shaped flowers from summer to fall
Color: golden yellow blooms
Height: 18 to 24 inches
Width: 18 to 24 inches
Light: full sun to light shade
Soil: well drained
Water: medium
Range: Zones 5 to 9
Remarks: native, drought-tolerant plant; likes fertilizer; will reseed; killed by frost; seedlings transplant easily

With its sunny flowers and bright foliage, the long-blooming, reliable melampodium fills out like a small shrub.

MONDO GRASS

❖

Ophiopogon japonicus

Plant type: evergreen ground cover
Landscape use: ground cover for shady areas
Features: deep green grassy foliage, grows into dense mat
Height: 4 to 8 inches
Form: spreading, grasslike
Texture: fine
Light: partial shade to full shade
Soil: any type
Water: medium
Range: Zones 7 to 9
Remarks: shear or mow in late winter if foliage is brown

Mondo grass is a neat evergreen ground cover that grows well under trees and offers a grasslike texture.

NANDINA

❖

Nandina domestica

Plant type: evergreen shrub
Landscape use: accent, border
Features: delicate foliage, summer flowers, profuse fall berries that last through winter
Color: white blooms, red or cream berries
Height: 1½ to 8 feet
Width: 3 to 4 feet
Form: upright, twiggy
Texture: fine
Light: full sun to shade
Soil: fertile, well drained
Water: low
Range: Zones 6 to 9
Remarks: durable despite delicate appearance, drought tolerant when established, great dwarf selections

Nandina's canelike stems boast clusters of red berries in the fall that are popular for holiday decorations.

OAK, LIVE

❖

Quercus virginiana

Plant type: evergreen tree
Landscape use: shade tree
Features: broad, spreading crown that casts dark, dappled shade; sculptural form
Height: 40 to 80 feet
Spread: 60 to 100 feet
Form: rounded, spreading
Texture: medium
Light: full sun
Soil: well drained
Water: medium
Range: Zones 7 to 10
Remarks: native, grows slowly, may live for 100 years or longer, tolerates salt spray

The long-lived, native live oak owes its grandeur to the spread of its massive limbs.

OAK, Willow

❖

Quercus phellos

Plant type: deciduous tree
Landscape use: shade or street tree
Features: impressive form, golden fall color
Height: 50 to 80 feet
Spread: 30 to 40 feet
Form: rounded to oval
Texture: fine
Light: full sun
Soil: moist, loamy, well drained
Water: medium
Range: Zone 7 to 9
Remarks: native, towering shade tree for city or home use

Willow oak grows into a large, rounded tree with the smallest leaves and finest texture of all the oaks.

Oleander is a sun-loving shrub that tolerates hot locations, poor, sandy soils, and even oceanside conditions.

OLEANDER, Common

❖

Nerium oleander

Plant type: evergreen shrub
Landscape use: accent, screen, mass planting, container plant
Features: profuse flowers from spring to fall, slender evergreen foliage
Color: white, pink, peach, or red blooms
Height: 6 to 12 feet
Width: 6 to 12 feet
Form: upright, rounded
Texture: medium
Light: full sun
Soil: rich, moist, well drained
Water: medium
Range: Zones 9 to 10
Remarks: very tolerant of heat, drought, and salt spray; may be perennial in Zone 8; poisonous leaves and fruit

PACHYSANDRA, JAPANESE

❖

Pachysandra terminalis

Plant type: evergreen ground cover
Landscape use: ground cover for shady areas
Features: lustrous, dark green whorled leaves; plush, elegant appearance
Height: 6 to 12 inches
Form: clumping
Texture: medium
Light: partial shade to full shade
Soil: rich, moist
Water: medium
Range: Zones 3 to 8
Remarks: does well over tree roots; spreads rapidly in soft, fertile topsoil

Japanese pachysandra forms a dense, elegant ground cover in shade.

PAMPAS GRASS

❖

Cortaderia selloana

Plant type: ornamental grass
Landscape use: accent, screen, mass planting, container plant
Features: fountainlike foliage; tall, feathery flower plumes in fall
Height: 6 to 10 feet
Width: 6 to 8 feet
Form: grasslike
Texture: fine
Light: full sun to partial shade
Soil: well drained
Water: low
Range: Zones 7 to 10
Remarks: evergreen in Zones 9 and 10, use brush cutter to cut back dense foliage

Once established, pampas grass reaches its full height in one season, so give it plenty of growing room.

PERIWINKLE, COMMON

❖

Vinca minor

Plant type: evergreen ground cover
Landscape use: ground cover
Features: glossy, narrow-leafed, deep green foliage; soft blue flowers in early spring
Height: 2 to 6 inches
Form: vining
Texture: fine
Light: partial shade to deep shade
Soil: rich, moist
Water: medium
Range: Zones 3 to 8
Remarks: mulch with compost to encourage rapid growth, cut back a mass planting with string trimmer

The early lilac-blue flowers of common periwinkle come to life when accompanied by daffodils and grape hyacinths.

PERIWINKLE, MADAGASCAR

❖

Catharanthus roseus

Plant type: annual
Landscape use: seasonal color
Features: nonstop flowers, drought tolerant
Color: white, pink, lavender, rose, or red blooms
Height: 3 to 20 inches
Width: 4 to 18 inches
Light: full sun to partial shade
Soil: slightly dry, poor
Water: low
Range: Zones 5 to 9
Remarks: often called vinca, good soil drainage essential, tolerates salt spray, newer selections are more susceptible to disease than old-fashioned types

Blooming profusely during the warm months, madagascar periwinkle tolerates hot, dry conditions and thrives on neglect.

Petunias will bloom for months if you trim off old flowers as they fade.

PETUNIA

❖

Petunia hybrids

Plant type: annual
Landscape use: seasonal color for beds and containers spring through fall
Features: trumpet-shaped flowers, eye-catching colors
Color: purple, white, red, pink, blue, lavender, salmon, or bicolored blooms
Height: 4 to 18 inches
Width: 4 to 36 inches
Light: full sun to light shade
Soil: well drained, fertile to poor
Water: low, wilts but comes back from drought
Range: Zones 5 to 9
Remarks: heat-tolerant types, such as Madness and Celebrity, last from spring until fall; old-fashioned types reseed

Flowering quince is a multibranched shrub whose flowers are the first to bloom at the earliest sign of spring.

QUINCE, FLOWERING

❖

Chaenomeles hybrids

Plant type: deciduous shrub
Landscape use: accent
Features: splendid late-winter or early-spring flowers
Color: white or salmon-red blooms
Height: 6 to 10 feet
Width: 6 to 10 feet
Form: upright, rounded
Texture: medium
Light: full sun to light shade
Soil: well drained
Water: medium
Range: Zones 4 to 9
Remarks: provides exquisite flowers in the garden

REDBUD

❖

Cercis canadensis

Plant type: deciduous tree
Landscape use: accent, patio tree
Features: bright, early-spring flowers; wide shape
Color: magenta or white blooms, gray bark
Height: 20 to 30 feet
Spread: 25 to 35 feet
Form: upright, spreading
Texture: medium
Light: full sun to partial shade
Soil: any type, well drained
Water: low to medium
Range: Zones 4 to 9
Remarks: native, tolerates heat and many types of soil, seedlings can be a nuisance

The native redbud gets its name from its colorful spring blooms.

ROSE, LADY BANKS

❖

Rosa banksiae

Plant type: evergreen vine
Landscape use: arbor or wall plant
Features: long, sprawling, thornless stems; yellow or white flowers in spring
Height: climbs 15 to 20 feet
Form: spreading
Texture: fine
Light: full sun to partial shade
Soil: any type, well drained
Water: low
Range: Zones 7 to 9
Remarks: grows quickly, needs support, white-flowered selection is fragrant

Lady Banks rose sprawls and cascades with spring flowers and delicate foliage.

ROSE-OF-SHARON

❖

Hibiscus syriacus

Plant type: deciduous shrub
Landscape use: accent, summer screen
Features: continuous flowers from late
  spring to early fall
Color: white, pink, or lavender blooms
Height: 8 to 12 feet
Width: 6 to 10 feet
Form: upright
Texture: medium
Light: full sun to partial shade
Soil: well drained
Water: medium
Range: Zones 5 to 9
Remarks: old-fashioned flowering shrub,
  tolerates poor soil

Old-fashioned Rose-of-Sharon, also known as althea, now includes improved selections such as this white Diana.

SAGO PALM

❖

Cycas revoluta

Plant type: palmlike evergreen shrub
Landscape use: accent, specimen, con-
  tainer plant
Features: rosettes of palmlike, glossy
  green leaves
Height: 5 to 7 feet
Width: 4 to 6 feet
Form: upright rosette shape
Texture: fine
Light: full sun to light shade
Soil: rich, well drained, acid
Water: low to medium
Range: Zones 9 to 10
Remarks: grows slowly; long-lived; use in
  pots in areas where it is not cold hardy,
  moving to a bright spot indoors in winter

Place the dramatic sago palm where it can serve as a garden accent.

SCILLA

Endymion hispanicus

Plant type: perennial (bulb)
Landscape use: accent, seasonal color, naturalizing
Features: drooping early-spring flowers, spiky foliage
Color: blue or lilac blooms
Height: 6 to 20 inches
Width: 8 to 12 inches
Light: full sun to partial shade
Soil: well drained
Water: low to medium
Range: Zones 2 to 8
Remarks: good plant for woodlands and borders

Scilla's delicate bell-shaped blooms are an attractive accent to a flowerbed or a woodland setting.

SOURWOOD

Oxydendrum arboreum

Plant type: deciduous tree
Landscape use: accent
Features: sprays of white late-summer flowers, deep red fall color, small stature
Height: 25 to 40 feet
Spread: 20 to 25 feet
Form: upright
Texture: medium
Light: afternoon shade
Soil: rich, well drained, acid
Water: medium
Range: Zones 4 to 8
Remarks: native, grows slowly

The beautiful scarlet color of sourwood is one of the first signs of autumn.

SPIREA, Bridal Wreath

Spiraea prunifolia

Plant type: deciduous shrub
Landscape use: accent, screen
Features: profuse early-spring flowers, bronze fall foliage
Color: white blooms
Height: 6 feet
Width: 5 to 6 feet
Form: upright, vase shaped
Texture: fine to medium
Light: full sun
Soil: rich, well drained
Water: medium
Range: Zones 3 to 9
Remarks: prune oldest canes to the ground every three or four years

Bridal wreath spirea is white when it blooms in spring, green in summer, and bronze as its leaves change color in autumn.

SPIREA, Reeves

Spiraea cantoniensis

Plant type: deciduous shrub
Landscape use: accent, mass planting, screen, natural hedge
Features: abundant spring flowers, delicate form
Color: white blooms
Height: 4 to 5 feet
Width: 4 to 8 feet
Form: arching, rounded
Texture: fine
Light: full sun
Soil: rich, well drained
Water: medium
Range: Zones 6 to 9
Remarks: long-lived, low maintenance, popular for flower arrangements

The loose, arching branches of Reeves spirea will quickly sprawl to fill a large space.

SWEET SHRUB, COMMON

❖

Calycanthus floridus

Plant type: deciduous shrub
Landscape use: naturalizing, border
Features: spring flowers, strawberry fragrance
Color: dark red or greenish yellow blooms
Height: 6 to 10 feet
Width: 6 to 10 feet
Form: rounded, multistemmed
Texture: medium to coarse
Light: full sun to light shade
Soil: any type
Water: low
Range: Zones 5 to 9
Remarks: easy to grow; colonizes by suckers; not all selections fragrant, Athens most fragrant

Although named for the fragrance of its spring flowers, sweet shrub is also noteworthy in the fall when its leaves turn golden yellow.

VERBENA, MOSS

❖

Verbena tenuisecta

Plant type: perennial
Landscape use: seasonal color for beds, borders, and containers
Features: mats of color from spring to fall, lacy foliage
Color: purple, white, or pink blooms
Height: 8 to 12 inches
Width: 48 to 72 inches
Form: spreading, creeping
Texture: fine
Light: full sun
Soil: well drained
Water: medium
Range: Zones 8 to 10
Remarks: remove spent blossoms for best show, trim to control spread

Even in hot, dry locations, moss verbena continues to bloom all summer long.

VIBURNUM, DOUBLEFILE

❖

Viburnum plicatum tomentosum

Plant type: deciduous shrub
Landscape use: large accent, foundation planting, small tree
Features: horizontal branches, dogwoodlike spring blossoms, showy red fruit
Color: white blooms, red fruit
Height: 5 to 15 feet
Width: 10 to 18 feet
Form: upright, spreading
Texture: medium
Light: full sun to partial shade
Soil: rich, well drained
Water: medium
Range: Zones 5 to 8
Remarks: shallow root system, grows rapidly once established

Doublefile viburnum produces an abundance of bright red fruit in late summer.

VIRGINIA CREEPER

❖

Parthenocissus quinquefolia

Plant type: deciduous vine
Landscape use: trellis, wall, or fence plant
Features: large, fanlike leaves; brilliant red fall color
Height: climbs to 30 feet
Form: climbing
Texture: medium
Light: full sun to partial shade
Soil: any type
Water: low
Range: Zones 3 to 10
Remarks: native, grows quickly, clings to masonry

The long vines of Virginia creeper can cover a wall or climb a tall tree.

WAX MYRTLE

❖

Myrica cerifera

Plant type: evergreen shrub
Landscape use: accent, screen, border, tree-form shrub
Features: bayberry-scented foliage
Height: 10 to 20 feet
Width: 15 to 20 feet
Form: upright, rounded
Texture: fine to medium
Light: full sun to partial shade
Soil: any type
Water: low to high
Range: Zones 7 to 10
Remarks: native, grows rapidly, tolerates dry or soggy sites, withstands salt spray

You can shear the native wax myrtle into a small tree or group several together to form an evergreen screen.

WISTERIA, American

❖

Wisteria frutescens

Plant type: deciduous vine
Landscape use: trellis, fence, or arbor plant
Features: drooping clusters of fragrant lavender flowers in late spring
Height: climbs 20 to 30 feet
Form: vining
Texture: medium to coarse
Light: full sun
Soil: moist, well drained
Water: low to medium
Range: Zones 6 to 10
Remarks: not as vigorous or invasive as Chinese wisteria, doesn't need fertilizer

American wisteria is a native vine that is less rampant and blooms a few weeks later than the Chinese wisteria.

YELLOW JESSAMINE

❖

Gelsemium sempervirens

Plant type: semievergreen vine
Landscape use: fence or trellis plant
Features: trumpet-shaped early-spring
   flowers
Color: yellow blooms
Height: climbs to 20 feet
Form: twining
Texture: fine
Light: full sun to shade
Soil: well drained, acid
Water: low to medium
Range: Zones 6 to 9
Remarks: native, fast growing, sporadic
   flowers in mild winters, poisonous if
   swallowed

A native vine, yellow jessamine tends to climb to the top of its support, while maintaining an open form at the base.

ZINNIA

❖

Zinnia elegans

Plant type: annual
Landscape use: seasonal color
Features: brilliant flowers from summer to
   fall, good for cutting
Color: white, orange, pink, red, yellow, or
   lavender blooms
Height: 12 to 36 inches
Width: 6 to 18 inches
Light: full sun
Soil: well drained, fertile
Water: low to medium
Range: Zones 5 to 9
Remarks: flowers quickly, attracts butter-
   flies, wide variety of types and sizes

Zinnias provide dependable, colorful blooms in the garden or in a cut-flower arrangement.

Plant Hardiness Zone Map

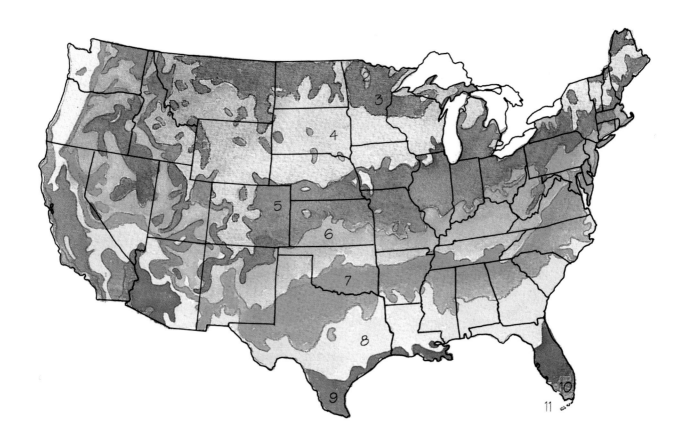

The United States Department of Agriculture has charted low temperatures throughout the country to determine the ranges of average low readings. The map above is based loosely on the USDA Plant Hardiness Zone Map, which was drawn from these findings. It does not take into account heat, soil, or moisture extremes and is intended as a guide, not a guarantee.

The southern regions of the United States that are mentioned in this book refer to the following:

Upper South: Zone 6

Middle South: upper region of Zone 7 (0 to 5 degrees minimum)

Lower South: lower region of Zone 7 and upper region of Zone 8 (5 to 15 degrees minimum)

Coastal South: lower region of Zone 8 and upper region of Zone 9 (15 to 25 degrees minimum)

Tropical South: lower region of Zone 9 and all of Zone 10 (25 to 40 degrees minimum)

	Zone 2	-50 to -40°F
	Zone 3	-40 to -30°F
	Zone 4	-30 to -20°F
	Zone 5	-20 to -10°F
	Zone 6	-10 to 0°F
	Zone 7	0 to 10°F
	Zone 8	10 to 20°F
	Zone 9	20 to 30°F
	Zone 10	30 to 40°F
	Zone 11	above 40°F

Index

Index

Special Thanks

Rebecca Bull Reed, Assistant
  Garden Design Editor,
  Southern Living magazine
Southern Living Custom Landscape
  Service (For information, call
  1-800-366-4712)
Chris Little, photograph,
  page 87 (top)
Jacqueline Giovanelli
Meredith Mathis
Cathy Ritter
Marty Slack
Southern Progress Corporation
  Library Staff